FAITH
Family Style

GENERATIONS GROWING TOGETHER

Writers: Angie Avers, Chip Borgstadt, Miriam Campbell, Rebecca Grothe, Jonette Knock, Sue Lennartson, Marilyn Miller, Diane Monroe, David Popple, David Renniger, Sunni Richardson, Linda Staats

Permissions, National Programs
Lutheran Brotherhood
625 Fourth Avenue South
Minneapolis, MN 55415

Permissions, Division for Congregational Ministries
Evangelical Lutheran Church in America
8765 West Higgins Road
Chicago, IL 60631

CONTENTS

FAITH FAMILY STYLE

FAITH FAMILY STYLE

WELCOME TO FAITH FAMILY STYLE!

This resource presents a new version of an age-old way to nurture faith. Families across the ages have passed along skills for building relationships, faith practices, and traditions from one generation to another through the experiences they share each day. Most congregations used to be like this as well, before age-segregated education classes became popular. Now, many congregations are seeking to recapture the richness of learning these skills and practices through experiences that include all generations.

Leaders of programs for children, youth, and families—in congregations, outdoor ministry sites, or other Christian communities—will find these tools in *Faith Family Style: Generations Growing Together*:

■ Encouragement to consider how effective intergenerational ministry can link together these three strands of emphasis: skills for living with others, practices that help us express and nurture faith, and the developmental assets;

■ Practical tips for leading intergenerational ministry and planning events that include all ages;

■ A Vision Points Workshop to guide a discussion among leaders and planners about total ministry with families in mind;

■ Ten complete session plans for fun, interactive events that gather all generations to grow in faith together.

WHAT IS FAITH FAMILY STYLE?

Imagine generations growing in faith together— what do you see? People of all ages worshiping together? Children and youth working alongside adults in a service project? Families pausing for a moment of prayer on their way out the door? Older adults and youth learning together? Children and adults playing a game?

What does it take to bring this picture to life? This resource invites you to consider three strands of emphasis that can work together to support a holistic ministry with children, youth, and families:

■ skills necessary for building strong relationships;

■ practices that help us express and nurture our faith;

■ the developmental assets.

Linked together as you plan programs, these strands promote the healthy relationships and practices necessary for people of all ages as they grow together in faith in your congregation or outdoor ministry site.

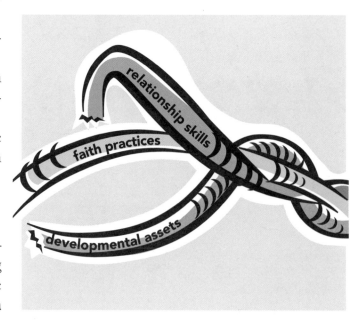

STRAND 1:
SKILLS FOR BUILDING STRONG RELATIONSHIPS

If asked to list all the skills necessary for creating and sustaining strong relationships, each of us probably could name many: listening, asking questions, telling one's own story, peaceful conflict resolution, honesty, standing up for one's convictions, serving the needs of another, empathy, making decisions, and so on. In the story of the Journey to Emmaus (Luke 24:13-35), we can glean additional insight into some key skills necessary for building a relationship with another person in God's family:

As they were talking and thinking about what had happened, Jesus came near and started walking along beside them. How can we challenge each other to expect to find Jesus present in the rhythms and questions of our everyday lives? We seek to see the presence of Jesus in our relationships with others who, like us, are seeking and exploring in their spiritual lives.

Jesus asked them, "What were you talking about as you walked along?" Jesus listened to the concerns of the disciples and drew them out. How can we encourage people to tell each other the stories of victories and challenges in their lives, and to explore God's presence in the midst of life?

Then Jesus asked the two disciples, "Why can't you understand? How can you be so slow to believe all that the prophets said? Didn't you know that the Messiah would have to suffer before he was given his glory?" At the right time, Jesus "got in their face" and clearly presented the truth. Truthful, loving feedback is an important part of any relationship. At the right time, we can help each other interpret our experiences in the light of the Gospel's promises.

They begged him, "Stay with us! It's already late, and the sun is going down." The disciples invited Jesus to spend time with them. Their hospitality to Jesus and to one another helped their relationships grow. Reaching out to others in hospitality can set the stage for new relationships.

After Jesus sat down to eat, he took some bread. He blessed it and broke it. Then he gave it to them. Around the table, Jesus and the disciples became companions. A companion is, literally, someone with whom we share our bread (*con panis* means "with bread"). The bread we share with others may be the bread of a meal or the Bread of Life shared in Holy Communion. Jesus is our companion in both circumstances.

So they got right up and returned to Jerusalem. The two disciples found the eleven apostles and others gathered together. Then the disciples from Emmaus told them what happened. The Emmaus disciples shared a relationship with the full company of disciples. They were accountable to the Body of Christ, so they returned to tell the news. One objective of building relationships is to help us, as God's children, grow in our ability to be accountable to the mission of the gospel and to share our faith with someone else.

Excerpts from *Companions on the Road: A Program of One-to-One Parish Mentoring,* copyright Evangelical Lutheran Church in America, Christian Education and Evangelism Team. www.elca.org/eteam/resources/mentors22.htm

Include this strand of emphasis in your intergenerational ministry programs by providing opportunities for participants of all ages to strengthen their own identity, learn new skills, practice rusty skills, and consider their own role in building strong relationships.

STRAND 2:
PRACTICES FOR EXPRESSING AND NURTURING FAITH

Dr. Martha Stortz, in *Faith Practices, Faith Lives: A Lutheran Perspective on Faith Practices,* describes faith practices as those "God-shaped and God-shaping activities that add up to a way of life." They are attitudes and actions that are rooted in scripture, but lived out in the world. Faith practices are how we "do faith" in our daily lives. They are the ways that Christians demonstrate their love for God, others, and themselves. By learning faith practices and participating in them many times over many years, individuals nurture their identity as children of God and grow as disciples.

The seven faith practices identified in the Evangelical Lutheran Church *Call to Discipleship* are:

- **Pray.** Individual and corporate prayer place us in the presence of God and allow us to intercede for our neighbor.
- **Study.** Study of the Bible and other faith-based writings introduces us to the world of many others in God's family and helps us better understand our own.
- **Worship.** In worship we acknowledge—and give thanks for—God's participation in our lives and offer ourselves in service.
- **Invite.** We are called to go and "tell what God has done for us," to live out inviting relationships with those who have yet to hear the gospel.
- **Encourage.** We encourage one another through speech, comfort, friendship, and striving together to understand our lives as God's children.
- **Serve.** The Holy Spirit sends us into the world to love and serve our neighbor.
- **Give.** We "offer with joy and thanksgiving" what God has given to us—time, talent, and treasure.

By putting an emphasis on how faith is lived, new Christians can learn what it means to live as a disciple. Those who have been members for a long time can be encouraged to renew their faith commitment by intentionally choosing to include certain faith practices in their own lives. And, perhaps most importantly, children and adults are given a pattern of daily activities that can help shape their identity and their values as a family of God's people. Include the strand of faith practices in your programs for intergenerational ministry so that people of all ages can find themselves participating with other faithful people in the work of God's grace in the world.

Excerpts from *ELCA Call to Discipleship, An Invitation to Participate,* by Paul Lutz. Copyright © 2000 Evangelical Lutheran Church in America. www.elca.org/init/teachthefaith/

STRAND 3:
THE DEVELOPMENTAL ASSETS

The developmental assets are positive experiences and qualities that young people need in order to be caring and responsible members of their communities. Search Institute of Minneapolis, with corporate support from Lutheran Brotherhood, developed this framework of 40 developmental assets based on its research with hundreds of thousands of young people. (There is a reproducible chart of the 40 assets on page 11 of this resource.) Young people from all backgrounds are more likely to be contributing, productive members of families, congregations, and communities when they have these assets in their lives. They also are less likely to become involved in violence, alcohol and other drug use, gambling, and other risky behaviors.

It is clear that children and youth need to experience support, care, and love from their families. Parents are the primary faith teachers and the primary asset builders. From the research done on the assets, we are reminded that children and youth also need caring and supportive relationships with other adults—extended family, neighbors, teachers, and congregation members. The more positive relationships with adults that a young person has, the better. The intergenerational ministry programs we plan can help these positive relationships grow.

Congregations and outdoor ministry sites are in a great position to build many of the assets in young people. They've been building these assets in young people for years! Being aware of the assets will not take away from the good things we do or displace the gospel-centered goals of the ministries we have with children, youth, and families. However, including this strand of emphasis in our intergenerational ministry will help more adults understand the importance of developing caring relationships with children and youth—caring relationships that can make it easier to nurture faith in each other.

Include the developmental assets to give some concrete, positive goals to the relationships that are grown through your intergenerational ministry programs.

MOVING FORWARD WITH INTERGENERATIONAL MINISTRY

- **First things first!** Create a vision of generations growing together. What do you want to see happening? Share your ideas with others as you strive to provide a full-service ministry with and for families. Plan to show the 10-minute video, "Faith Family Style," to adult and youth classes and groups to spark their imagination as you begin this conversation. Also, the Entry Points for Ministry Workshop on page 13 has suggestions for guiding a discussion about your vision.

- **Be inclusive!** Promote practical ways for people of all ages to become actively involved in worship, education, fellowship, and service together.

- **Be intentional!** Maximize the potential of your programming. Plan activities that will strengthen families and engage people of all ages and encourage them to build relationships with one another.

- **Be perceptive!** Tune into new information about how people learn to help you better honor each person's emotional, spiritual, and intellectual needs and development.

- **Work to affirm!** Honor the needs and characteristics of each generation. Look for ways to affirm and involve people of all ages in your faith community.

- **Make generations growing together a priority!** Invite each adult and young person to get to know each other. Also, share information about the asset framework and urge everyone to work at including these positive life building blocks in their relationships.

PRACTICAL TIPS FOR USING THE TEN EVENT PLANS

✔ Each of the ten plans for intergenerational events in this book will provide activities for a two-hour event. They can be adapted or expanded to fit your time and your setting. If you are leading these events as part of a full-day or weekend retreat, you probably will want to combine two or more plans, while still allowing plenty of time for music, meals, recreation, and worship.

✔ Make sure that single people know that they are important members of God's intergenerational family and encourage them to participate in the events. Emphasize that the relationships they form with young people are essential to nuturing God's family in your faith community.

✔ The activities in the event plans generally are not suitable for children under the age of five. Arrange loving child care for these younger ones, encouraging them to join their families during music activities, mealtimes, and breaks.

✔ Consider using the ten programs as monthly intergenerational gatherings or a weekly evening gathering during the summer months.

✔ As you schedule the events, consider how the event themes might highlight scripture texts you are studying.

✔ Plan how these events can take place in settings in addition to your regular classrooms or meeting rooms. Get people up and moving and outside, whenever possible.

✔ Explore ways that congregations and outdoor

ministry sites can partner to plan and host intergenerational retreats or special events based on one or more of the ten event plans.

✔ Share the leadership tasks for the events—find co-planners to direct publicity, gather supplies, serve as event leader, facilitate small group activities, coordinate child care, and organize cleanup. Remember to include youth as leaders, too!

✔ If intergenerational events are new to your group, try personal invitations as well as printed or spoken announcements. Describe or demonstrate an activity to help people know what to expect. Remember to get the word out about your events at least five times in at least three different ways.

RESOURCE LISTING

Church and Family Together: A Congregational Manual for Black Family Ministry (Valley Forge, Pennsylvania: Judson Press, 1996.)

Collins, Gary, *Family Shock: Keeping Families Strong in the Midst of Earthshaking Change* (Wheaton, Illinois: Tyndale House Publishers, Inc., 1995.)

Dumke, Miriam Campbell, *Take It To Heart: Nurturing Children, Youth and Families in Faith Community* (Minneapolis, Minnesota: Evangelical Lutheran Church in America and Lutheran Brotherhood, 1997.)

Gambone, James V., Ph.D., *Intentional Intergenerational Ministry: A Starter Kit* (Minneapolis, Minnesota: Lutheran Brotherhood, 1998.)

Garland, Diane R., *Family Ministry: A Comprehensive Guide* (Downers Grove, Illinois: InterVarsity Press, 1999.)

Rainer, Thomas S., *The Bridger Generation* (Nashville, Tennessee: Broadman and Holman Publishers, 1997.)

Roehlkepartain, Gene, *Building Assets in Congregations: A Practical Guide For Helping Youth Grow Up Healthy* (Minneapolis, Minnesota: Search Institute, 1997.)

Roehlkepartain, Jolene, *Building Assets Together: 135 Group Activities for Helping Youth Succeed* (Minneapolis, Minnesota: Search Institute, 1998.)

Thompson, Marjorie, *Family the Forming Center: A Vision of the Role of Family in Spiritual Formation* (Nashville, Tennessee: Upper Room Books, 1996.)

What NeXt: Connecting Your Ministry to the Generation Formerly Known as X (Minneapolis, Minnesota: Augsburg Fortress Publishers, 1999.)

THE 40 DEVELOPMENTAL ASSETS

DEVELOPMENTAL ASSET	HOW FAITH COMMUNITIES MIGHT NURTURE THIS ASSET
1. **Family support**—Family life provides high levels of love and support.	Inspire and equip families to provide unconditional love and support.
2. **Positive family communication**—Young person and her or his parent(s) communicate positively, and young person is willing to seek advice and counsel from parent(s).	Provide opportunities to learn and model skills for healthy communication and grace-filled conflict resolution.
3. **Other adult relationships**—Young person receives support from three or more nonparent adults.	Encourage members of all ages to be actively involved in fulfilling their baptismal promise to welcome, encourage, and support children and their parents as members of God's family. Encourage them to form positive relationships with young people in their neighborhood, too.
4. **Caring neighborhood**—Young person experiences caring neighbors.	Plan programs and train people to show care and concern for children and youth in the congregation, surrounding neighborhood, and community.
5. **Caring school climate**—School provides a caring, encouraging environment.	Support the efforts of your local schools to provide a caring and encouraging environment for children to learn and grow.
6. **Parent involvement in schooling**—Parent(s) are actively involved in helping young person succeed in school.	Lead or sponsor parenting classes that include ideas for actively supporting the educational growth and development of children.
7. **Community values youth**—Young person perceives that adults in the community value youth.	Welcome children and youth as needed and valued members of your faith community.
8. **Youth as resources**—Young people are given useful roles in the community.	Identify the interests, talents, and abilities of children and youth and nurture them through a variety of opportunities for leadership and involvement.
9. **Service to others**—Young person serves in the community one hour or more per week.	Provide intergenerational and age-specific ways to nurture the heart of a servant in your congregation and community.
10. **Safety**—Young person feels safe at home, school, and in the neighborhood.	Nurture a sense of security with policies that prescribe safety in programming, volunteer recruitment, and leadership training.
11. **Family boundaries**—Family has clear rules and consequences and monitors the young person's whereabouts.	Make a congregational commitment to interpret faith in real and relevant ways. Family or intergenerational workshops model and convey the importance of roles, boundaries, expectations, and accountability in family life.
12. **School boundaries**—School provides clear rules and consequences.	Affirm the need for schools to give children consistent expectations and accountabilities and strive to do the same in your own programs.
13. **Neighborhood boundaries**—Neighbors take responsibility for monitoring young people's behavior.	Encourage adult members of the congregation to consider it their responsibility to affirm and monitor the behavior of children in their congregation, neighborhood, and community.
14. **Adult role models**—Parent(s) and other adults model positive, responsible behavior.	Challenge parents and other adults to model lifestyles and behaviors that are healthy, mature, and responsible.
15. **Positive peer influence**—Young person's best friends model responsible behavior.	Affirm responsibility and age-appropriate maturity as assets that reflect characteristics of discipleship. Encourage youth to be positive role models.
16. **High expectations**—Both parent(s) and teachers encourage the young person to do well.	Make sure that programs and relationships inspire a desire in people to aspire to be all that God has gifted them to be.
17. **Creative activities**—Young person spends three or more hours per week in lessons or practice in music, theater, or other arts.	Provide and promote opportunities to develop artistic, dramatic, and musical talents, interests, and abilities.
18. **Youth programs**—Young person spends three or more hours per week in sports, clubs, or organizations at school and/or in the community.	Provide and support programs that are effectively engaging families in the healthy development of their God-given interests and abilities.
19. **Religious community**—Young person spends one or more hours per week in activities in a religious institution.	Devote well-planned programs with family-friendly schedules to nurturing faith in real and relevant ways. Create a strong partnership between the church and the home.

DEVELOPMENTAL ASSET	HOW FAITH COMMUNITIES MIGHT NURTURE THIS ASSET
20. Time at home—Young person is out with friends "with nothing special to do" two or fewer nights per week.	Model and promote healthy lifestyles that include constructive family time along with rest and recreation or leisure.
21. Achievement motivation—Young person is motivated to do well in school.	Find ways to support children and youth in their school work. Replace a focus on competition to "be the best" with an ongoing inspiration to "do their God-given best."
22. School engagement—Young person is actively engaged in learning.	Encourage families to be active and enthusiastic participants in age-specific and inter-generational learning programs.
23. Homework—Young person reports doing at least one hour of homework every school day.	Provide or promote after-school programs, study halls, or tutoring services to nurture academic accountability.
24. Bonding to school—Young person cares about her or his school.	Encourage children and youth to be active participants in their schools; keep members informed of school activities.
25. Reading for pleasure—Young person reads for pleasure three or more hours per week.	Build a strong church library to provide books and other resources to develop literary skills and provide inspiration and guidance for faithful living.
26. Caring—Young person places high value on helping other people.	Invite families to become involved in intergenerational opportunities to help people in need.
27. Equality and social justice—Young person places high value on promoting equality and reducing hunger and poverty.	Plan for opportunities for learning and responding to local and global hunger, poverty, and issues of injustice.
28. Integrity—Young person acts on convictions and stands up for her or his beliefs.	Nurture a sense of belonging and identity to God's family and inspire an inner strength and commitment to act accordingly.
29. Honesty—Young person "tells the truth even when it is not easy."	Provide learning opportunities for all members to grow in their desire, confidence, and commitment to speak the truth in love.
30. Responsibility—Young person accepts and takes personal responsibility.	Stress that children and youth are accountable to God, to themselves, and to others.
31. Restraint—Young person believes it is important not to be sexually active or to use alcohol or other drugs.	Foster a growing awareness and commitment to a lifestyle that is Christ's style—empowering children, youth, and families to refrain from unhealthy sexual and drug-related behavior.
32. Planning and decision making—Young person knows how to plan ahead and make choices.	Build a desire in children and youth to plan ahead and make good choices. Engage young people as partners in planning and leadership in the congregation.
33. Interpersonal competence—Young person has empathy, sensitivity, and friendship skills.	Use 1 John 3:16-18 to inspire children and youth to model friendship, empathy, and sensitivity to others.
34. Cultural competence—Young person has knowledge of and comfort with people of different cultural/racial/ethnic backgrounds.	Plan intergenerational activities, cultural expressions of worship and song, global mission festivals, and interpretations of scripture that encourage an understanding and appreciation of age, gender, culture, and ethnic diversity.
35. Resistance skills—Young person can resist negative peer pressure and dangerous situations.	Equip children and youth with the skills, confidence, and strength that only God can give to resist peer pressure and potentially dangerous situations.
36. Peaceful conflict resolution—Young person seeks to resolve conflict nonviolently.	Provide opportunities for children and youth to learn peaceful, practical, grace-filled ways to encounter and resolve conflict.
37. Personal power—Young person feels he or she has control over "things that happen to me."	Challenge children and youth to grow in their understanding of Philippians 4:13.
38. Self-esteem—Young person reports having a high self-esteem.	Value children and youth as baptized, loved, and forgiven children of God.
39. Sense of purpose—Young person reports that "my life has a purpose."	Give children and youth age-appropriate opportunities to discover their God-given potential and nurture a growing sense of purpose or vocation.
40. Positive view of personal future—Young person is optimistic about her or his personal future.	Teach age-appropriate interpretations of Hebrews 12:1-2b: "We must keep our eyes on Jesus, who leads us and makes our faith complete." Empower children and youth to be optimistic about their future.

ENTRY POINTS FOR MINISTRY WORKSHOP

A PLAN FOR LEADING A DISCUSSION OF TOTAL MINISTRY WITH FAMILIES IN MIND

WHAT IS A FAMILY?

Families are the most fundamental and influential of all institutions. The fabric of our society is maintained and sustained by the roles families play in everything from procreation and identity formation to learning routine daily tasks. As we know, there seems to be an ever-growing number of family configurations and household dynamics in our society today. However, it's intriguing to keep in mind that Joe Leonard and Richard Olson list 40 implied and identified family types in biblical times in *A New Day For Family Ministry* (Bethesda, Maryland: The Alban Institute, 1996).

Jesus spent little time commenting on any ideal concept of a family. He considered their strengths, challenges, and needs as he reached out and embraced them. Jesus used relevant and relational ways to teach the faith and to inspire faith to flow into every aspect of the daily lives of all families that he touched.

Our call to ministry remains the same today. We are called to grow in our commitment to nurture families in faith and community. Jesus' model for ministry also challenges us to set goals for approaching our faith-nurturing work in practical and holistic ways. After all, faith is not nurtured in a vacuum!

In his explanation to the Third Article of the Apostle's Creed, Martin Luther focuses on the amazing role of the Holy Spirit to call, gather, enlighten, and sanctify the whole Christian church on earth. The activity of the Spirit is reflected in the many common and ordinary ways that we nurture faith. The gifts of the teacher, the topic or biblical text, the students' interests and abilities, the relationships in the group, and the setting of the learning all come together to create the educational experience.

Congregations and outdoor ministry sites, eager to nurture *faithful* disciples, are challenged to attend to the ways in which they energize and equip *faith* to *flow* into every aspect of the daily lives of the baptized. They are challenged to weave together the strands of skills necessary for building strong relationships, the practices that express and nurture faith, and the developmental assets.

ENTRY POINTS FOR MINISTRY

This workshop introduces five vision points to consider as you establish and interpret family ministry as a perspective rather than a separate program. They can help you interpret your total ministry as "family" ministry. Each vision point invites you to explore your total ministry with families in mind as:

✔ a priority that flows through every program in your congregation or outdoor ministry site;

✔ an opportunity to strengthen relationships among generations by nurturing relationship skills, faith practices, and developmental assets;

✔ a lens through which programs are planned and visions for ministry are established;

✔ a motivation for interpreting faith in relational ways;

✔ an active partnership between the Christian community and the home.

Use these five vision points as a self-study guide. Better yet, invite other planners and leaders to discuss them with you. You could explore one vision point per meeting over a period of time or plan for a two-hour session to discuss all of them. This workshop could be a great way to plan for the coming year. Arrange a time to view the video, "Faith Family Style," with your planners to inspire them to participate in a discussion of vision points.

VISION POINT #1:

As we embrace people of all generations as vital members of our faith community, our ministries will reflect a working knowledge of and sensitivity to the presence of many lifestyles and family configurations.

GETTING STARTED

Scan through the most recent membership directory from your congregation or the congregations you serve as an outdoor ministry site. If you don't have one, think about who was at the last worship service you attended.

Reflection:

1. Who do you see in the church directory? What impressions does it give you about the family dynamics of your faith community?

2. How many members of each family do you really know? What do you know about them? Do they have specific areas of involvement?

3. Based on what you see, how would you define *family*?

INSIGHTS TO CONSIDER

■ The Census Bureau defines family as two or more persons related by birth, marriage, or adoption residing together.

■ William Sheek, author of *The Word on Families: A Biblical Guide to Family Wellbeing* (Abingdon Press, 1988), defines family from a faith perspective, "We, as sisters and brothers in the family of God, accept equally as families those who are related by marriage or remarriage, blood or adoption; those who covenant to live together as family; and those single persons and persons living alone who choose to be family with others outside their kinship families."

■ Jesus ministered to many families. He did not belabor how they were configured, but affirmed them and addressed their most practical needs as an entry point for nurturing them in faith and community.

INSPIRATION

I kneel in prayer to the Father. All beings in heaven and on earth receive their life from him.

Ephesians 3:14-15

INVITATIONS FOR MINISTRY

■ Pray for each family unit. Ask God to give you a passion for embracing each one as vital and significant members of God's family.

■ Plan a time to review data that will give you a more complete picture of the family dynamics represented in your faith community. You can get demographic data from the Census Bureau, your county, and your Chamber of Commerce.

Your synod office may also have access to data that will assist you.

- Imagine the needs that families might have for personal, social, and spiritual support. Assess the ability of your current programming to nurture, welcome, and engage individuals of all ages in your faith community.

- Follow the lead of one pastor who provided three entry points for engaging people of all ages in a worship service. Each component of the service was introduced with a child-friendly reference first, then an instructional one, followed by a practical one. For example, "This is the part of the service when we think of all the mistakes we've made and need to tell God we're sorry. It's called the Confession and it's found on page 77."

VISION POINT #2:

AS WE EMBRACE PEOPLE OF ALL GENERATIONS AS VITAL MEMBERS OF OUR FAITH COMMUNITY, OUR MINISTRIES WILL WELCOME AND ENGAGE FAMILIES, AFFIRM THEIR STRENGTHS, AND ADDRESS THEIR ONGOING NEEDS FOR NURTURE AND SUPPORT.

GETTING STARTED

Gather an envelope (any size) and a blank piece of paper. On the back of the envelope, draw a simple portrait of the people you would consider your immediate family. Surround the portrait with things about your family that are known or readily observed, such as your address, the kind of car you drive, your family configuration, pets you have, involvement in athletic teams, and so on.

Next, rip the blank paper into several small pieces and write down something on each one that is more personal in nature. Include things that shape your family from within, such as dreams, fears, needs you're striving to satisfy, challenges, or

ongoing conflicts. Place the pieces of paper in the envelope and tuck in the flap.

Reflection:

1. What connections are there between the picture on the outside of the envelope and the slips of paper inside? Would people who know your family be surprised by what you wrote on the slips? How do you balance the personal and public aspects of your life? Think about the sense of continuity, support, and community you feel.

2. Expand this exercise to consider the known and unknown realities that shape any family. Does your congregation or outdoor ministry site model a climate of unconditional love, acceptance, and community? Does it provide a variety of programs for engaging, supporting, empowering, and equipping people of all ages as they encounter the joys and challenges of life?

INSIGHTS TO CONSIDER

- There are three basic needs that are common to all people: a positive identity and sense of belonging, a meaningful opportunity for growth and involvement, and a sense of purpose or vocation.

- We all have a depth within us that longs to be filled and it will...with something. It is the unique privilege of the church to fill it with the love, hope, identity, and sense of community that only God can give.

INSPIRATION

God is wonderful and glorious. I pray that his Spirit will make you become strong followers and that Christ will live in your hearts because of your faith. Stand firm and be deeply rooted in his love. Ephesians 3:16-17

INVITATIONS FOR MINISTRY

- List the unique gifts and abilities that members of each generation bring to the task of building a healthy faith community. (For example, young children bring curiosity and easy smiles; elders bring rich stories to tell.) As you make the list, refer to the first 20 developmental assets, listed on page 11, for ideas of how these gifts and abilities might be expressed in community.

■ Assess the ability of your current program ministries to engage and empower people of all ages with the skills, confidence, and commitment to nurture their dreams, address uncertainties, and cope with challenges.

VISION POINT #3:

AS WE EMBRACE PEOPLE OF ALL GENERATIONS AS VITAL MEMBERS OF OUR FAITH COMMUNITY, OUR MINISTRIES WILL INSPIRE FAMILIES TO SEE SIGNS OF GOD'S ACTIVITY AND PRESENCE IN THEIR DAILY LIVES AND STRENGTHEN THEIR ABILITY TO COPE WITH LIFE'S CHALLENGES AND UNCERTAINTIES.

GETTING STARTED

Reflect on the drawing below and visualize God's amazing regard for people as you read the following passages:

I often think of the heavens your hands have made, and of the moon and stars you put in place. Then I ask, "Why do you care about us humans? Why are you concerned for us weaklings?" You made us a little lower than you yourself, and you have crowned us with glory and honor. You let us rule everything your hands have made. And you put all of it under our power.

Psalm 8:3-6

I will bless you with a future filled with hope—a future of success, not of suffering.

Jeremiah 29:11

God has given us many resources with which to live our lives fully and faithfully. Make note of some

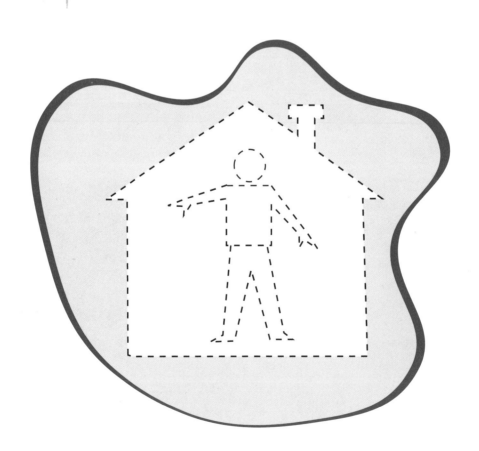

of the gifts, talents, and personality traits that God has given you. Write them inside the outline of the person. Identify some of the relationships and resources that accommodate your needs. Write them inside the outline of the home. Finally, acknowledge some of the realities, challenges, or waves of influence that have shaped your dreams and altered your good intent. Write them on the wavy lines that surround the home.

After you complete this exercise, read the story of Peter (Matthew 14:22-33) and consider it from your own perspective. Ask yourself where Jesus is in the midst of the adventures in your life. Then, consider which one of the following statements best describes your feelings about your current situation:

■ My faith and commitment to follow Jesus enable me to navigate the waves and help me keep my eyes on him.

■ I'm overwhelmed by the waves and my own limitations—I'm just barely staying afloat.

■ I'm treading water, and hoping that God will give me the strength to continue.

■ I'm just bobbing at random, looking for someone or something to bale me out.

Reflection:

1. Imagine other families you know. Would they consider your congregation or outdoor ministry site to be a strong source of inspiration and support for facing the challenges of life or just one of the many waves of influence in their lives?

2. How do your current ministries nurture a trust and confidence in Jesus? Do they help families see signs of God's presence and activity amidst the challenges of life? What skills are you teaching to help people of all ages cope?

INSIGHTS TO CONSIDER

Six qualities of strong families identified by Nick Stinnett and John Defrain in *Secrets of Strong Families* (Little Brown, 1985):

1. **Commitment.** Members are dedicated to promoting each other's welfare and happiness. They value the unity of the family and are committed to one another and to the family group.

2. **Appreciation.** They express appreciation for each other.

3. **Communication.** They have good communication skills and spend a lot of time talking with each other.

4. **Time together.** They spend considerable amounts of quality time together.

5. **Spiritual commitment.** They have a high degree of commitment and strong faith expression. Most belong to organized churches and have a religion that is a personal, practical, day-to-day experience rather than something theoretical.

6. **Coping ability.** They have the ability to cope with crises, bad times, and stress in a positive way that helps them grow.

INSPIRATION

I pray that you and all of God's people will understand what is called wide or long or high or deep. I want you to know all about Christ's love, although it is too wonderful to be measured. Then your lives will be filled with all that God is.

Ephesians 3:18-19

INVITATIONS FOR MINISTRY

■ Teach the basics of Christian faith and nurture characteristics of discipleship in every area of ministry. The Evangelical Lutheran Church in America identified seven faith practices that are integral components of a living faith: pray, study, worship, give, encourage, invite, serve. Additional information about these is available at www.elca.org/init/teachthefaith/index.html.

■ Lead, sponsor, or make referrals to individual and family programs for practical support and recovery. "Ways to Nurture Faith through Life Transitions" is a series of articles that provides practical ways for faith communities to welcome and uphold families when they encounter specific challenges. Find them at www.elca.org/eteam/resources/lifetransit.htm.

■ Establish a strong prayer ministry.

VISION POINT #4:
AS WE EMBRACE PEOPLE OF ALL GENERATIONS AS VITAL MEMBERS OF OUR FAITH COMMUNITY, OUR MINISTRIES WILL HONOR INDIVIDUAL LEARNING STYLES AND PROVIDE AGE-APPROPRIATE OPPORTUNITIES FOR NURTURING FAITH THAT WILL FLOW INTO EVERY ASPECT OF OUR DAILY LIVES.

GETTING STARTED

Sing or read one of these hymns that include rich images of God and our relationship with God: "How Marvelous God's Greatness" (*Lutheran Book of Worship, 515*); "My Soul, Now Praise Your Maker" (*Lutheran Book of Worship, 519*); "Immortal, Invisible, God Only Wise" (*Lutheran Book of Worship, 526*).

Reflection:

1. What images of God and faith are nurtured in your faith community?
2. Does your congregation or outdoor ministry site provide occasions for inquiry, dialogue, and response to basic questions of faith and uncertainties?
3. How do you consider age-level characteristics and individual learning styles as you plan lessons and activities?
4. Identify some of the ways you encourage expressions of faith to flow through individual talents, thoughts, and activities.

INSIGHT TO CONSIDER

Edgar Dale, in his research that led to his Cone of Experiences (1960), identifies how the manner in which individuals receive information is related to what they retain. For example, people generally remember:

- 10% of what they read;
- 20% of what they hear;
- 30% of what they see;
- 50% of what they hear and see;
- 70% of what they say and write; and
- 90% of what they say as they do a task.

INSPIRATION

Listen, Israel! The LORD our God is the only true God! So love the LORD your God with all your heart, soul, and strength. Memorize his laws and tell them to your children over and over again. Talk about them all the time, whether you're at home or walking along the road or going to bed at night, or getting up in the morning.

Deuteronomy 6:4-7

INVITATIONS FOR MINISTRY

- Provide occasions for families and broader intergenerational groups to share their life stories and faith stories with each other. Consider video and audio taping sessions to record interviews.
- As you plan to use the ten event plans in this resource, read through the practical tips on page 9 and think about how you will create the setting for intergenerational growth and involvement.
- Provide and promote programs that nurture the imagination and artistic expressions of faith, such as vocal and instrumental lessons or choral groups, drama groups, and art activities.
- Assess how well the printed resources you use in your programs support your vision of how children, youth, and adults grow as disciples.

VISION POINT #5:

AS WE EMBRACE PEOPLE OF ALL GENERATIONS AS VITAL MEMBERS OF OUR FAITH COMMUNITY, OUR MINISTRIES WILL BE SHAPED BY OUR COMMITMENT TO LIFELONG LEARNING AS WE DESIGN PROGRAMS THAT TEACH FAITH SKILLS AND PERSPECTIVES IN RELEVANT AND RELATIONAL WAYS.

GETTING STARTED

Think back to the last time there was a baptism in a worship service you attended. What commitments were made by the parents and the congregation? Baptism is an amazing entry point for faith growth in community. But it may leave families wondering, "What's next? What is it all supposed to mean?"

The parents are to take primary responsibility for teaching the child the Ten Commandments and the Lord's Prayer, to place in his or her hands the Holy Scriptures, and to bring their child to worship.

The congregation celebrates newly baptized children as members of God's family and invites them to come and work with them in the kingdom of God. And, as they do these things, the child is to shine so that the world may see his or her good works and glorify the Father who is in heaven. Now this task may sound pretty simple. But, it doesn't take long before it becomes necessary to break it down into play-by-play strategic moves to uphold everyone's good intent.

Reflection:

1. What programs do you have in place that nurture a desire for lifelong learning? How many of them incorporate intergenerational involvement?

2. How do Christians of all ages in your outdoor ministry site or congregation engage, empower, and equip parents to fulfill their primary roles as faith teachers?

3. What is the strength of the connection between your Christian community and the homes of its members?

4. How do members of all generations grow together in faith in your midst?

INSIGHTS TO CONSIDER

■ *"Most certainly father and mother are apostles, bishops and priests to their children, for it is they who make them acquainted with the gospel. In short, there is no greater or nobler authority on earth than that of parents over children, for this authority is both spiritual and temporal. Whoever teaches the gospel to another is truly his apostle or bishop."*

Martin Luther,
Treatise on the "Estate of Marriage"

■ One study clearly demonstrates that life experiences are strongly associated with maturity of faith. Having family and friends are two near-universal experiences that have impact on one's growth in faith maturity. As each of the specific experiences listed below increases, so also does faith maturity. On many of these factors, large percentages of adolescents reported little or no involvement. For example, among ELCA youth:

■ 35% rarely or never talked to mother about faith or God between ages 5 and 12;

■ 57% rarely or never talked to father about faith or God;

■ 69% rarely or never talked to other relatives about faith or God;

■ 44% rarely or never talked to best friends about faith or God;

■ 68% rarely or never participated in family projects to help others.

Effective Christian Education: A National Study of Protestant Congregations—A Report for the Evangelical Lutheran Church in America. (Search Institute, 1990)

INSPIRATION

You have taught me since I was a child, and I never stop telling about your marvelous deeds. Don't leave me when I am old and my hair turns gray. Let me tell future generations about your mighty power. You have taught me ever since I was young, and I still tell of your wonderful acts. Now that I am old and my hair is gray...be with me while I proclaim your power and might to all generations to come.

Psalms 71:17-18

INVITATIONS FOR MINISTRY

■ Examine one program from your ministry. Identify the many factors involved in creating its learning environment.

■ Look through the list of the 40 developmental assets and ideas for how they can be nurtured in a faith community on page 9. Which ones are you already addressing in your programs? Which ones do you want to nurture more effectively? How could relationships among generations be strengthened through your programs?

■ Plan how you will use the ten event plans in this book to strengthen relationships among generations. How can these events serve as entry points for nurturing faith in relational ways among all generations?

■ Revisit each of the Vision Points and summarize your ideas and plans for shaping a total ministry with families in mind.

End your Vision Points Workshop by joining in *"A Blessing for Families"* found on page 21.

A BLESSING FOR FAMILIES

Leader: Since the first embrace of "one, with another," individual dreams and schemes have given life and breath to many versions of the community we call family.

Reader 1: Even as part of Adam was taken to make Eve, a plan accompanied their reason for being. God created amazing inspiration and support for them as he urged them to establish dominion over all living things and provide for the overall stewardship of the earth; not to mention the intriguing invitation God gave them to be fruitful and multiply.

Group: *Such is the mystery of marriage.*

Reader 2: Sarah laughed as she and Abraham tried to fathom God's timing for expanding their family.

Group: *Such is the overwhelming blessing of managing the joys and challenges of children, no matter when we begin.*

Reader 3: The sibling rivalry between Mary and Martha inspired Jesus to help them clarify their boundaries, expectations, and priorities.

Group: *Such is the challenge of nurturing faith in daily life.*

Reader 4: The stable accommodations weren't exactly five-star and the long haul to Egypt hardly vouched for the arrival of a king.

Group: *Such is the need for faith in God's presence and guidance, though we cannot always see it.*

Reader 5: Peter didn't struggle with God's invitation to walk alone across the water until he felt the wind and became overwhelmed with the waves.

Group: *Such are the ongoing realities of venturing out on our own.*

Reader 6: Ruth and Naomi's life transitions challenged them to renew and redefine their future.

Group: *Such is the reality of dealing with the loss of loved ones.*

Leader: For this reason I bow my knees before the Father from whom every family in heaven and on earth takes its name. I pray that, according to the riches of his glory, he may grant that we each be strengthened in our inner beings with power through the Spirit, and that Christ may dwell in our hearts through faith, as we are being rooted and grounded in love. I pray that we may have the power to comprehend with all the saints what is the breadth and length and height and depth, and to know the love of Christ that surpasses knowledge, so that we may be filled with all the fullness of God.

Group: *O Lord, you have searched us and known us. You know when we sit down and when we rise up. You search out our paths and our lying down, and you are acquainted with all our ways. Even before a word is on my tongue, O Lord, you know it completely. Where can I go from your spirit? If I take the wings of the morning and settle in the farthest part of the sea, even there your hand shall lead me, and your right hand shall hold me fast.*

Leader: We thank you for the amazing and assuring gift of your love and presence through baptism. As we mark the beginning of new life in our community within your family we retrace the sign of the cross on our foreheads to celebrate the identity we share, the individual gifts we have to offer and the privilege of reflecting your good intent for families. Amen.

(Each person is invited to dip a finger in the bowl of water and make the sign of the cross on her or his forehead.)

Reader 7: Thank you, Lord, for creating families and the unique individuals that give them life and breath. We are humbled by your presence, power, and activity in our lives. It reminds us that no matter what life brings, you promise to hold us in your firm and mighty hands.

Group: *May the Lord bless and keep our families. And as his face shines upon us, keep us from being distracted by other fleeting pleasures. Let us be as humbly thankful as God is gracious. And help us to receive the peace God so wants to give us.*

Leader: In the name of the Father, and the Son, and the Holy Spirit. Amen.

FAITH SHAPERS

DISCOVER WHAT GIVES SHAPE TO LIFE AND FAITH

THIS INTERGENERATIONAL EVENT LINKS:

- The skills for telling one's personal story;
- The practice of worship (giving thanks); and
- Asset 39, Sense of Purpose.

KEY LEARNING POINTS

✔ As part of God's family, our faith is shaped by our stories and by the stories of those around us.

✔ Learning about the faith stories of others in God's family can help us imagine a sense of purpose for our lives.

✔ We help each other give thanks for the strong foundation of God's presence in the circumstances of everyday life.

BACKGROUND FOR THE LEADER

In contemporary culture, there are many influences that shape the lives of children, youth, and families: lifestyles, relationships, opportunities for learning and empowerment, the level of safety in one's neighborhood, media, community, and the church. In this session, participants will share their stories with each other about some of these influences. As stories are shared, remember to affirm the church as the foundation that gives one purpose in life, rather than just another wave of influence in shaping our lives.

Intergenerational teams are an essential part of this session. Working in teams with persons of many ages helps participants understand the importance of relationships in shaping a vibrant faith. Members of the faith community give shape to each person's sense of their purpose as a member of the Body of Christ. In this session, strive to build appreciation for the relationship-building skills of telling one's story.

📖 KEY BIBLE TEXTS

Stand firm and be deeply rooted in his love. I pray that you and all of God's people will understand what is called wide or long or high or deep. I want you to know all about Christ's love, although it is too wonderful to be measured. Then your lives will be filled with all that God is.

Ephesians 3:17b-19

Anyone who comes and listens to me and obeys me is like someone who dug down deep and built a house on solid rock. When the flood came and the river rushed against the house, it was built so well that it didn't even shake. But anyone who hears what I say and doesn't obey me is like someone whose house wasn't built on solid rock. As soon as the river rushed against that house, it was smashed to pieces!

Luke 6:47-49

EVENT SCHEDULE

Let's gather	**20 minutes**
Making faith connections	
Living stones	25 minutes
Break	10 minutes
ABCs of faith	20 minutes
House plaques	15 minutes
Prayer stones	15 minutes
Closing	**15 minutes**

MATERIALS NEEDED

Let's gather
- 40 index cards
- Play dough in four different colors, one golf-ball-size piece per person

Living stones
- 2 small stones, about the size of a quarter, for each person

ABCs of faith
- Chart paper and markers

House plaques
- Cardboard patterns for hearts in three sizes: 6", 5", and 4"
- Cardboard pattern of simple house shape, no larger than 2" x 2"
- Poster board in a variety of colors
- glue, scissors, markers

Prayer stones
- Small stones from the "Living Stones" activity
- Hot glue gun
- Markers

Closing
- Bibles, worship books

PREPARATION

- Tend to the ministry of hospitality by providing name tags and making sure that there is comfortable seating for all participants.
- Purchase play dough in four colors or use a recipe to make some.
- Make card sets for the gathering activity. Prepare one set of cards for every eight persons.

  Card Set A: Top card should say: "Arrange the cards to spell out Ephesians 3:17b." Then write each word of this verse on its own card: Stand firm and be deeply rooted in God's love.

  Card Set B: Top card should say: "Arrange the cards to spell out Luke 6:47." Then write this verse on the cards, two words per card: Anyone who/ comes and/ listens to/ me and/ obeys me/ is like/ someone who/ dug down/ deep and/ built a/ house on/ solid rock.

- On chart paper, print these phrases in large letters for the "Living Stones" activity:
  - Someone who helped you see God's action
  - Favorite Bible story
  - Favorite hymn, camp song, or Sunday school song
  - Time when it's hard to have faith
  - Time you told someone about Jesus
  - Time you felt God's love
  - Why it is important to go to church
  - How you stay connected to God each day
- Bring a snack for the break time.
- For the "ABCs of Faith" activity, write the letters of the alphabet down the left-hand side of a sheet of chart paper. Make one sheet for each team of 6-8 participants.
- Make a completed "House Plaque" as an example for participants. See the illustration with the activity instructions.
- Make copies of the reproducible sheet that follows this session. Use a heavy weight of color paper or card stock. Cut apart so that each participant has two cards. Make a completed card as a sample.

LET'S GATHER (20 MINUTES)

As participants arrive, welcome them and encourage them to put on a name tag.

Team sculpture

Give each person a piece of play dough about the size of a golf ball. Have participants gather into teams that have the same color of play dough. (Be sensitive to families who want to stay together; let them trade colors with others so they can be on the same team.) Tell each team to stand in a circle. The person whose birthday is closest to that day begins to create a sculpture of any object that he or she chooses. Next, tell participants that they are to add to the sculpture with their balls of dough when it is their turn. Send the sculpture around their circle, allowing each person 15 seconds to add to the sculpture. After each team member has contributed to the shape, gather the sculptures from each team and put them on a table.

Ask the group: "Did your sculptures turn out the way you were hoping they would?" Allow time for a few responses. Conclude by saying: "Many hands shaped the sculptures you made, and there were a few surprises! There are many things that shape our lives and our faith, too. We'll take a look at some of these things today."

Build a verse

Form teams of six to eight people, making sure there are people from different generations on each team. Give each team one set of the cards you prepared earlier. Say: "In your teams, work together to put the cards in order as directed on the top card of the stack. Be sure to listen to each other and ask everyone on the team to help."

Allow three minutes for teams to complete their task. Ask each team to read aloud together the verse

they constructed. Point out that these verses remind us of the importance of letting God and God's word be important shapers in our lives.

Ask the group: "How does it feel working in teams of different ages? What surprised you?" Allow time for a few responses. Summarize your two gathering activities by saying, "As part of God's family, our faith is shaped by those around us, even as we shape their faith. We need each other to help us shape faith-filled lives and faith-filled families. God has given us each other as wonderful gifts."

Pray something like, "Creator God, we thank you for the gift of each person in this room. Help us to shape each other in loving and faithful ways. Help us grow to know you better as we share our stories and our questions. Amen."

MAKING FAITH CONNECTIONS

Living Stones (25 minutes)

Purpose: To learn from each other's faith experiences and strengthen one's sense of purpose in life as God's child.

Ask several volunteers to distribute the small stones, two per person. Ask for another volunteer to read aloud Luke 6:47-49. Tell the group that Jesus spoke these words. Comment: "Listening to the teachings of Jesus shapes us in powerful ways. Faith gives each one of us a solid foundation for living, as solid as these rocks. Our lives are shaped by our faith each day."

Show the group the chart paper you prepared earlier with the thought starter phrases. Say: "If we listened to one person tell a story about each of these in her or his life, we would know a lot about how faith has been a life shaper for her or him."

Explain that in this next activity, each person will have time to tell a story about how faith has been an important shaper in his or her life.

Ask participants to return to the teams that constructed the Bible verses. In their teams, participants will take turns giving a response or telling a short story for two of the thought starters, one for each of their stones. As participants share their stories, they add their stones to a team pile of stones.

Allow 15-20 minutes for this sharing time. Tell teams when they are five minutes from the completion time. When the teams are finished, ask them to bring their stones to one large pile for the group. Say: "We help each other find God's presence in the circumstances of everyday life as we share our faith stories. Hearing the stories of other believers helps us shape our own lives. This helps each one of us grow a stronger sense of purpose in our own lives. Having a strong sense of purpose is a key building block, or asset, for healthy development. It is important that we spend time together, learning from each other, sharing our faith stories, and thanking God for his loving presence in our everyday activities. When we do, our stories connect to create a solid foundation for our faith community."

Break (10 minutes)

ABCs of Faith (15 minutes)

Purpose: To work together to name relationships, circumstances, and activities that nurture a strong faith.

Have participants stay in the same teams from the last activity. Give each team some markers and one sheet of the chart paper that you prepared earlier with the letters of the alphabet. Instruct them to

think of a word that describes a relationship, a person, a circumstance, or an activity that helps us grow in faith for each letter of the alphabet. The letter of the alphabet can appear anywhere within the word. (For example, "A" could be hAving a role model, bAptism, or Aunts who pray for us.)

Allow seven minutes for the teams to record their words. Encourage groups to move on to the next letter if they get stuck on one. They can always return to the letter later.

After you call time, ask teams to post their chart paper on the wall and to sit close to it. Starting with the letter A, ask each team to share their faith word. If more than one team suggests the same word for letter A, only the first team to say it can count it. All other teams who have that word must cross it out. Let teams take turns giving their word first. After all 26 letters have been shared, have teams total up the number of words they have that are not crossed out. Affirm all groups as they share their score, and offer a round of applause for the team with the highest score.

Say: "As part of God's family, our faith is shaped by those around us. And each one of us helps to shape the faith of others in God's family. In our teams today, we thought of dozens of ways our faith grows each day. And we have a strong connection with each other in every one of those ways. We can tell our faith stories. We can be strong role models for each other. We can encourage each other to do our best. We need each other if we are going to grow stronger in our faith and closer to God."

House Plaques (15 minutes)

Purpose: To create a visual reminder of Luke 6:47-49.

Create a work area with the three sizes of heart patterns, house pattern, scissors, glue, and markers. Have a completed plaque as a reference point for participants. Tell the group that sometimes we need something to remind us of how much God's love shapes our lives. Each household will make a reminder to take home.

To make a plaque:

- Using the three heart patterns, cut one of each size from poster board in any colors you choose.
- Using the house pattern, cut one from any color of poster board.
- Glue the four pieces together, starting with the largest heart and ending with the house.
- Write the name(s) of each person who lives in the household inside the house shape.
- Along the edge of the bottom heart, print the verse reminder: God's love is our foundation.
- A paper clip can be taped to the back as a hanger, if desired.

God's love is our foundation.

Prayer Stones (15 minutes)

Purpose: To encourage participants to reach out to others with the message of God's love.

Create a work area with the small stones used earlier in the session, markers, a glue gun, copies of the reproducible sheet you made earlier, and a completed card as a sample.

Comment on how important it is to tell others the stories about how God's love has shaped our lives. These "Prayer Stones" cards can help us begin that conversation. Each person will make two cards, one to give away and one to keep.

To make a Prayer Stones card:

- Use markers to draw a cross on a stone.
- Glue the stone to a card created from the reproducible sheet.
- Sign the card and add other messages or decorations as desired with markers.

As a group, thank God for each of the recipients of these cards. Encourage participants to remember to pray for the person who receives their Prayer Stone card each time they see the Prayer Stone card that they have kept.

Closing (15 minutes)

Begin your closing time by saying something like: "There are many things that influence how our faith is shaped. We give thanks that God has given us our Baptisms and each other in the church as a foundation for faithful living. As we live and grow together, we encourage each other to take our faith into our daily lives. Ephesians 4:11-13 says that Christ chose some of us to be apostles, prophets, missionaries, pastors, and teachers, so that his people would learn to serve and his body would grow strong. This will continue until we are united by our faith and by our understanding of the Son of God. Then we will be mature, just as Christ is, and we will be completely like him. Christ has given us all gifts to help each other grow in faith. It is part of our purpose in life to use our gifts to offer thanks to God."

Ask participants to form teams of five or six persons. Tell each team they will have five minutes to plan one way to express their thanks for others in the body of Christ and the way that God uses them to help strengthen our faith. Have Bibles and worship books available. (Ideas may include: offering a prayer, leading a song, performing a short skit, or reading a scripture.)

After five minutes, have the entire group gather in an area where all can be seated. Ask each team to offer what they have prepared in the presence of the whole group.

Finally, summarize the three key learning points:

- As part of God's family, our faith is shaped by our stories and by the stories of those around us.
- Learning about the faith stories of others in God's family can help us imagine a sense of purpose for our lives.
- We help each other give thanks for the strong foundation of God's presence in the circumstances of everyday life.

Close with a prayer like:

"Loving God, you have given us each other to help us grow in faith. Open our eyes to see your love in the actions of our families. Open our ears to hear your words in the stories of our friends. Open our hearts to experience your love as we share with those in our communities. Influence us—and let us be influences for others—as we live thankful lives in your gracious love. Amen."

ME TALK? TO GOD?

CLAIM POSITIVE COMMUNICATION AND PRAYER

THIS INTERGENERATIONAL EVENT LINKS:

- The skills necessary for daily conversation;
- The faith practice of prayer; and
- Asset 2, Positive Family Communication.

KEY LEARNING POINTS

- ✔ We can grow in our skills for positive communication within our families.
- ✔ The ways in which we communicate with each other can influence how we pray.
- ✔ Prayer in its many forms is our way of communicating with God.

📖 KEY BIBLE TEXTS

My dear friends, you should be quick to listen and slow to speak or to get angry...My dear friends, with our tongues we speak both praises and curses. We praise our Lord and Father, and we curse people who were created to be like God, and this isn't right.

James 1:19; 3:9-10

BACKGROUND FOR THE LEADER

Verbal communication is an integral part of who we are. The average person speaks up to 40,000 words a day, give or take a few. The messages that others receive from us are more complex than mere words. Only 7% of the complete message that the other person receives are the words we speak. Fifty-eight percent of the message that is nonverbal—our gestures and body posture—and the remaining 35% of the message is relayed through our tone of voice. The task of communicating with another person is made even more complex because while the maximum number of words we can speak per minute is limited to around 125, our minds can process up to 400-600 words per minute. This enables our listener to "read between the lines" and adapt or interpret our words.

Our communication skills influence the shape of our lives and relationships. Asset 2, Positive Family Communication, is a reminder to us that communicating positively and seeking advice from one another are powerful building blocks in the development of children and youth, as well as adults. Members of the faith community who strive for positive communication among family members are powerful faith-shaping resources.

Our daily interactions with each other also shape our understanding and involvement in prayer! After all, prayer is communicating with God. With this in mind, the intent of this event is to explore the dynamics of positive communication in the home and in the larger family of God as a premise for deepening a desire for meaningful prayer.

📚 EVENT SCHEDULE

Let's gather	**15 minutes**
Making faith connections	
Create a conversation	**10 minutes**
Special effects	**10 minutes**
Now you're talkin'!	**25 minutes**
Break	**10 minutes**
God Talk blocks	**25 minutes**
Closing	
Prayer T.I.P.S.	**25 minutes**

MATERIALS NEEDED

Let's gather
- Washable markers: red, yellow, green, blue
- Mouth puppet reproducible sheet on page 35

Create a conversation
- Chart paper, markers

Now you're talkin'
- Chart paper, markers
- Construction paper
- Skit script from page 36

Break
- Large red apples, one for every four persons
- Sharp knife or apple slicer
- Softened cream cheese or peanut butter
- Miniature marshmallows, about 8 per person

God Talk Blocks
- 1-1/2" or 2" wooden blocks, one per household
- 2" squares of fine sand paper, one per household
- Fine-line permanent markers in the following colors: red, brown, blue, green, yellow, black
- Very small adhesive bandages
- Pencils
- God Talk Block User Guide reproducible sheet

Prayer T.I.P.S.
- Pretzel twists (not sticks)
- Chart paper, markers

PREPARATION

- Tend to the ministry of hospitality by providing name tags and making sure that there is comfortable seating for all participants.
- Make one copy of the mouth puppet reproducible sheet on page 35 for each participant. Make a puppet as a sample.
- On a sheet of chart paper, make a chart of this code using your four colors of washable markers:
  Red = Hi
  Blue = How are you?
  Green = Just fine
  Yellow = Thank you
- On a sheet of chart paper, write these phrases:
  Cliche
  Reporting facts about other people and things
  Sharing personal thoughts and opinions
  Sharing personal feelings and emotions
  Open, honest, and intimate conversations
- Print each of these words on its own sheet of construction paper: strangers, acquaintances, friends, best friends, family members, God.
- Make one copy of the God Talk Block User Guide reproducible sheet on page 37 for each household unit. Make a block as a sample.
- Make four copies of the skit script on page 36. Ahead of the event, recruit four volunteers to act this out for the group.
- On a sheet of chart paper, write these phrases:
  T = Thank you
  I = I'm sorry
  P = Praise
  S = Special needs and requests

> Throughout this session, small groups are called teams to differentiate them from the large group. Whenever you see the term *group*, it refers to all the teams together.

LET'S GATHER (15 MINUTES)

As participants arrive, welcome them and encourage them to put on a name tag. Use washable markers to make one colored dot on the palm of everyone's hand. Alternate using red, yellow, green, and blue markers so you have about the same number of people with each color of dot. (This is preparation for the "Create a Conversation" activity.)

Give participants copies of the mouth puppet sheets and markers. Ask them to jot down in the mouth some of the cliche words or phrases and common topics they hear people using today—both people they know and people in the media. After they have made a few notations, encourage children and adults to work together to fold the design along the dotted lines, accordion-style, to make mouth puppets. Place one hand behind the middle fold to make the mouth go open and shut.

Introduce yourself to the group using the mouth

puppet and ask participants to take a turn doing the same, including their name and their favorite word or phrase to say. If you have a large group, do these introductions in teams of five or six people.

In the large group, engage participants in a brief discussion using the following questions as a guide.

1. To whom do you usually talk?
2. When and where do you usually talk with them?
3. What do you usually talk about?

Tell participants that during this event, you'll take a look at some of the ways we talk to God and each other.

MAKING FAITH CONNECTIONS

Create a conversation (10 minutes)

Purpose: To better understand the role each person plays in communication.

Refer to the chart that has the code for the dots you have placed on the palm of each person's hand. Tell them that the object of this game is for participants to search for people who can help them create a complete conversation. When you give the start signal, participants will wander around whispering the word or phrase associated with their colored dot. When they encounter someone who says a phrase that usually comes right after their word or phrase, they should link arms and continue their search together, saying both their phrases. When they have found all the people they need to create the entire conversation, tell them to cheer and sit down as a group.

Comment: "Each person had a key part of your

ASSET 2: Positive Family Communication. Young person and her or his parent(s) communicate positively, and young person is willing to seek advice and counsel from parents. In your congregation, this asset can be nurtured by providing opportunities to learn and model skills for healthy communication and grace-filled conflict resolution.

---

complete communication. We need to give full attention to the words other people are saying as we seek to share messages and get things done. And it's important to be able to do this in positive ways!"

Special effects (10 minutes)

Purpose: To explore the role of nonverbal cues and tone of voice in communication.

Say, "The words that we say are just one part of the way that we communicate. In fact, when we communicate with another person, words make up only about 10% of the message that the other person receives. Almost one third of the actual message is shaped by our tone of voice and two thirds by our body language. This exercise will give you an opportunity to see how tone of voice and face or body expressions affect what we hear when people speak."

Invite everyone to choose a partner and stand face to face. Have participants take turns repeating a phrase after you, using a tone or emotion that you designate. For each phrase, give them one of these emotions: sarcasm (sassiness), sadness, great joy, frustration or anger, no emotion at all. Use these phrases:

- Hello there.
- Nice job.
- Thank you.
- Finally, you're here!
- How can I help you?

Conclude this exercise by asking participants to comment to each other on what they observed or experienced, using this question to guide the discussion: How did facial expressions, hand motions, and body positions make a difference in how we interpreted what was being said?

Ask a volunteer to read aloud James 3:9-10. Offer a prayer that God will inspire your conversations today.

Now you're talkin'! (25 minutes)

Purpose: To learn more about types of communication and imagine how they are connected to one's prayer life.

Gather in the large group. Say: "The average person says up to 40,000 words a day. We talk about different things with different people. There are five different types of communication that we often use."

Ask two adult or older youth volunteers to read each of these short dialogues to illustrate each of the types before you present the information about it. Refer to the chart you made as you briefly explain each one.

Cliche

Person #1: Hi!

Person #2: Hi! How are you?

Person #1: Just Fine. How are you?

Person #2: Fine. Thank you.

Explain that this is an example of cliche, greetings and comments made in passing, or surface talk. It makes up 90% of our communication.

Reporting facts about others

Person #1: Did you hear about the Hancocks? They went to Disney World!

Person #2: When did they go?

Person #1: Last Friday.

Person #2: Did they drive or fly?

Person #1: They drove.

Person #2: How long will they be gone?

Person #1: Ten days.

Explain that this is reporting facts about other people and things, including the weather, news, and current events.

My thoughts and opinions

Person #1: Well, I think that's a pretty long time to take kids out of school just to see Cinderella's castle!

Person #2: The trip in itself could be an adventure in learning.

Person #1: Nothing can take the place of a math problem or a spelling word.

Person #2: I think I'd create spelling lists using the names of Disney characters and the town and state they live in.

Person #1: Not in my lifetime!

Explain that this is sharing personal thoughts and opinions about news and events.

My feelings and emotions

Person #1: I'd love to go to Florida at this time of year.

Person #2: I'd hate to drive all that way!

Person #1: Well, with that attitude, I don't think I'd enjoy riding with you all that way!

Person #2: I'm just not into watching Snow White dancing around all her little dwarfs.

Explain that this is sharing personal feelings and emotions.

Open, honest, and intimate communication

Person #1: I'm wondering why you have such strong feelings about Disney World.

Person #2: Well, when I was six, I used to pretend I was Peter Pan all the time. I had this great outfit and a little stuffed Tinkerbell—you know, the fairy—pinned to my shoulder. Anyway, once when I went shopping with my mom with my outfit on, my friend Mary Lou saw me and she said, "Hey, can I have some fairy dust so I can fly, too?" After that, every time she saw me, she'd say, "Don't you know that fairy tales are just for people who look like Prince Charming or want to get kissed?" I'd get so embarrassed, I decided I was going to stay as far away from fairy tales and imaginary characters as I could.

Person #1: Thanks for telling me. I can understand why you feel the way you do. Wouldn't it be fun, though, if you could give your kids the feeling that it's OK to enjoy make-believe characters and imaginary play?

Person #2: Maybe it would help me let go of Mary Lou's comments, too.

Explain that this was an example of open, honest, and intimate conversation, a time when you can share whatever is in your heart and mind without reservation.

Ask participants to make teams of four or five persons each. Have them discuss this question in their teams: "When do you use each of these types of communication in your own lives?"

Next, hold up each of the construction paper signs you made, pausing after each one for team discussion. Hold up the "God" sign last. Ask teams to talk about the type of communication that people are most likely to have with each of the individuals or groups named on the signs. Show the "God" sign and ask them to identify the type of communication they are most apt to use when they talk with God.

Ask participants to gather again in the large group. Draw an empty cartoon conversation "bubble" on a piece of chart paper. Inside, print: Prayer is _____. Ask participants to call out some of the common prayers they have prayed, like table prayers, bedtime prayers, the Lord's Prayer, etc. Write their responses around the outside of the conversation bubble. Next, invite participants to suggest ways to fill in the blank in the phrase, "Prayer is _____." Summarize their comments by printing "talking to God" on the line.

Introduce the skit, "Conversations with Rex," thanking the volunteers who are acting in it for bringing a message to the group. After the skit, ask participants to comment on whether they agree or disagree with the mother's last comment and why.

Break (10 minutes)

If you like, make apple smiles for break. Cut apples into eight wedges each. Plan on two wedges for each participant. Lay the first of each section on its side and spread cream cheese or peanut butter on it. Stick mini marshmallows along the outer edge of the slice to resemble teeth. Then, spread the other section and place it on top of the marshmallows. It should be positioned to look like a smile.

God Talk Blocks
(25 minutes)

Purpose: To create a visual reminder of the importance of prayer and to encourage more prayer at home.

Place paper towels, wooden blocks, sand paper, sharp scissors, index cards, and permanent markers on a resource table.

Hold up the finished block you made as a sample and tell the group that it can be a tool to help people strengthen communication and prayer in their homes. Comment that this little block, used with the user guide sheet, can prompt conversation and prayer on a variety of different levels.

Give each household unit a copy of the God Talk Block User Guide sheet and refer to it as you demonstrate how the block is used:

- Identify the symbols on the six faces of the block as the topics suggested on the sheet.
- **Table Talk.** Conversation starters for when people are gathered, i.e. at mealtime.
- **Faith Talk.** References to God and faith-related concepts in our conversations about people and events in our lives.
- **Bible Talk**. Verses we can share from the Bible that relate to each topic.
- **God Talk.** Ideas to start prayers related to the topic.

Demonstrate how the block can be used. Toss it and show the side that landed face up. Then show how to find the row on the chart that matches the picture on the block and move across the row, talking about each of the thought starters in that row, and closing with prayer.

Suggest that these blocks might be placed on their kitchen tables to prompt communication and prayer during meals, as 90% of all family communication takes place during meal time. The block may also be used to guide one-on-one conversations and individual prayer.

Instructions for making the blocks:

1. Sand the wooden block until it's smooth.
2. Carefully copy the pictures from the side of the God Talk Block User Guide onto each side of the block with a pencil.
3. Use permanent markers to color the shapes on each side of the block. Place a bandage on the broken heart.
4. Encourage participants to practice tossing the block and using their user guide charts to start conversations with each other while everyone has a chance to finish their blocks.

CLOSING

Prayer T.I.P.S. (25 minutes)
Purpose: To focus a time of prayer for others. Review the key learning points of this session:

■ We can grow in our skills for positive communication within our families.
■ The ways in which we communicate with each other can influence how we pray.
■ Prayer in its many forms is our way of communicating with God.

Point out that God wants us to share our thoughts and feelings about our lives, the good things and the difficult times, our mistakes, and the desires of our hearts in prayer. God also wants us to include the joys and special needs of others.

Introduce the following tool to help people of all ages share their many thoughts and concerns with God. Suggest that every time they pray silently or aloud they can use the following "tips" to help them remember specific prayers to pray.

T = "Thank you" prayers for people, things, and experiences we really appreciate.
I = "I'm sorry" prayers for mistakes we make.
P = Praise prayers about God's awesome love, power, and activity in our lives.
S = Special requests for help and healing for self and others.

Invite everyone to join you in a circle outside, around a campfire, or indoors, around a candle. Hold up a bowl of pretzels and ask participants to try to make their arms the shape of a pretzel. Mention that a long time ago people used to fold their arms into the shape of a pretzel when they prayed. Some monks made unleavened bread in the shape of a pretzel during the season of Lent to remind people to pray.

Invite everyone to keep their arms in the shape of a pretzel as you prepare to close your meeting in prayer. Before words are spoken, remind them that listening is also an important part of communication. In Psalm 46:10 it says, "Calm down, and learn that I am God!"

To quiet the group and prepare for prayer, choose one of these options:

1. Play a recorded song or have someone sing a song that talks about God's great goodness.
2. Observe 60 seconds of silence and invite participants to reflect on God's presence and activity in their lives.

Then, use the prayer T.I.P.S. and invite group members to offer petitions for each of the prayer topics. End your prayer time with a benediction:

May the Lord bless us and keep us,
May God's face shine upon us,
May God's blessing go with us
And give us peace.
Amen.

Characters: Narrator, Rex Smith, Rex's Father, Rex's Mother

Props: Two phones, a chair, a tablet of paper and pen, appropriate hats (*if desired*)

Narrator: For many years Rex Smith had held the belief that when a person was grown and living far from his parental home, he should make an effort to keep in touch with the people who brought him into this world. Therefore, once a week, he placed a phone call to his parents' home in a distant part of the country. If his father answered, Rex would say...

Rex: (*Picks up the phone and speaks in a robotic, monotone voice*) My father who lives in Toledo, may your name be held in high esteem. May your days come, may your work get done."

Narrator: If his mother answered the phone, Rex would recite...

Rex: (*Picks up the phone and speaks in a robotic, monotone voice*) Now I call you before I sleep. I hope your health you still do keep. If I should die before I wake, I hope you miss me for my sake.

Narrator: His routine never varied. He didn't say anything more or anything different. Again and again his parents tried to break into his speeches, but each time he kept going until he finished. Then he hung up. His parents had questions they wanted to ask him and things they wanted to tell him, but Rex never took time for anything but his recitation. His parents wrote to him, saying...

Parents: (*Mother using pen and pad*) We love you. We want to know how things are going for you. Communicate with us--please!

Narrator: Rex paid no attention to their letters. Then, one day as he was half way through his routine...

Rex: Now I call you before I sleep...

Narrator: He sneezed and lost his place... (*Rex sneezes.*)

Rex: If I should die. If I should die. If I should die. (*Keeps repeating it until the end of the play.*)

Mother: Rex! Listen to me!

Narrator: His mother tried to shout over his voice but it was no use. Rex kept repeating the same words over and over and over and over. Finally, his parents quit trying to get through to him and hung up the phone.

Mother: (*Sinking into a chair as her husband pats her shoulder*) It's really sad! Some people talk to their parents the way they talk to God!"

GOD TALK BLOCK USER GUIDE

Topic	Table Talk	Faith Talk	Bible Talk	God Talk
	What's something you've been thinking about today?	Name gifts that you are glad God has given you.	*Every good and perfect gift comes down from the Father who created all the lights in the heavens.* James 1:17	Thank God for your own life and the lives of those around you.
	What's going on in the world today?	Name needs you see for God's help and our assistance.	*God loved the people of this world so much that he gave his only Son, so that everyone who has faith in him will have eternal life and never really die.* John 3:16	Pray for God's help and guidance for yourself and for others in the world.
	Tell where you've been today and the people you were with.	What signs did you see of God's presence or activity?	*Always let [God] lead you, and he will clear the road for you to follow.* Proverbs 3:6	Pray that God will guide your steps.
	Who is hurting or suffering today?	Name some ways that God and others can help those in distress.	*God cares for you, so turn all your worries over to him.* 1 Peter 5:7	Pray for God's healing and love, shown through others.
	What good news or personal accomplishment do you have to share today?	What ability or experience has God provided in your life?	*Shout praises to the LORD, everyone on this earth. Be joyful and sing as you come in to worship the LORD!* Psalm 100:1-2	Give thanks and praise to God for the good things in your life, this day and all days.
	What mistakes or disappointments were part of your day?	What advice or reassurance might God's word give?	*But God showed how much he loved us by having Christ die for us, even though we were sinful.* Romans 5:8	Confess the wrong that has been done this day and ask for God's forgiveness.

AT YOUR SERVICE

DEVELOP THE HEART OF A SERVANT

This intergenerational event links:

- The skills of perceiving the needs of others and opportunities for service;
- The faith practice of serving our neighbor; and
- Asset 9, Service to Others.

KEY LEARNING POINTS

- ✔ We learn about servanthood from Jesus.
- ✔ Four ways to serve are: do, give, pray, speak.
- ✔ We can be more aware of opportunities for service—globally, in the community, at school or work, and in the congregation.

📖 KEY BIBLE TEXTS

Then Jesus asked, "Which one of these three people was a real neighbor to the man who was beaten up by robbers?" The teacher answered, "The one who showed pity." Jesus said, "Go and do the same!"

Luke 10:36-37

BACKGROUND FOR THE LEADER

No matter where people go in the world, they will observe or experience people who are serving others. Driving through a fast food restaurant, people take our orders and prepare food for us. Police and emergency technicians, as well as government officials, are known as public servants. Children and parents help each other at home. Global neighbors provide food and other products for our use.

As Christians we are called to care for the needs of others. God has given each person gifts, passions, interests, and abilities for service. As people discover their strengths, they can more effectively choose areas of service to express their love and faith. This intergenerational event will focus on Jesus' ministry as the model for servanthood. The activities will help participants learn more about their own gifts for serving and about the importance of service opportunities in the healthy development of young lives.

🗒 EVENT SCHEDULE

Let's gather	
Beginning activities	**10 minutes**
Opening celebration	**15 minutes**
Making faith connections	
Gifted to serve	**25 minutes**
Break	**10 minutes**
Service stations	**35 minutes**
"Send Me" towels	**15 minutes**
Closing	**10 minutes**

MATERIALS NEEDED

Beginning activities

- Construction paper in assorted colors, two 9" squares per person
- Pencils, scissors, markers
- Safety pins, two per person
- Index cards, 20 cards for every eight persons

Opening celebration

- Chart paper, markers
- Hymnals or songbooks

Gifted to serve
- Gifted to Serve reproducible sheet on page 44
- Masking tape

Break
- Snack item of your choice

Service stations
- Materials will depend on the activities chosen. See page 42 for activity suggestions

"Send Me" towels
- Plain cotton fabric, one 10" x 16" piece for each participant. Option: one sheet of 9" x 12" construction paper for each participant, fringed with scissor cuts at one end
- Supplies for decorating towels, such as markers, rubber stamps, stickers, fabric scraps
- White glue, scissors

Closing
- Bible
- Candles and matches
- Pitcher of water, basin, towel
- Song books or hymnals for participants

PREPARATION

- Well ahead of your event, choose two or three activities for each service station, as described on page 42. Gather the materials required. You may want to put a list of materials needed in the bulletin and ask for donations. You also could ask participants to bring some materials with them. Recruit four Service Station attendants to help participants review the way of serving that is the focus of the station and to coordinate the activities there.
- As you read through the plan, consider appropriate leaders for specific tasks. If possible, pair a child with an adult or older youth. You need: greeters to welcome participants and assist with the beginning activities; Service Station attendants; worship leaders—readers, song leader, skit participants.
- Identify 12 ways that people serve in your outdoor ministry site, congregation, or community. Print each service opportunity on two index cards (so that there is a pair of cards that

match). Try to include opportunities that represent all four ways of serving: do, give, pray, speak. For example, read the lessons in worship, lead games at family camp, pray for missionaries, donate food to Loaves and Fishes, talk to member of city council about need for stop sign at a dangerous intersection, etc. Make one set of these cards for every eight participants.

- Use markers to design a large cross banner on chart paper. Label each arm of the cross with one of the following words: Do, Give, Pray, Speak. Post this banner in a prominent location.
- Plan an area for the opening and closing that allows participants to sit in a circle or semi-circle. If possible, gather in a space that has a cross.
- Make a copy of the Gifted to Serve reproducible sheet on page 44 for each participant.
- Make signs to label each Service Station area. (You could invite a youth to do these on a computer.)
- Pray for a fun, spirit-filled experience for participants and enthusiastic leaders.

> **Throughout this session, small groups are called teams to differentiate them from the large group. Whenever you see the term *group*, it refers to all the teams together.**

LET'S GATHER

Beginning activities (10 minutes)

Purpose: To introduce participants to each other and to the theme of the event.

Lend A Hand

Lay out construction paper squares, pencils, markers, scissors, and safety pins. Ask participants to trace their own hands, cut them out, and write their

names in the palms. Each person will make two name tags. Encourage them to wear both name tags, attaching them with safety pins. Tell them that one of the name tags will be used during the closing worship.

At your service!

Set up enough places to play so that participants are in groups of no more than eight. For each game, mix up a set of the index cards you prepared earlier and place them face down on the table.

Direct participants to a playing area after they complete their nametags. Tell them that this game will get them thinking about the many ways that people in their outdoor ministry site or congregation and their community serve others.

Directions for the game:

The first player randomly chooses two cards and turns them face up. If the service opportunities match, the player picks them up and keeps them. If they don't match, the cards are turned face down again. Continue play in this way with each person in the group. The game ends when all the matches have been made.

Opening celebration (15 minutes)

Purpose: To join in prayer, praise, and Bible study on the theme.

Welcome participants, and sing one or two familiar songs. Refer to their name tags as you ask participants to identify things that we do with our hands to help other people. After you have acknowledged a few activities, suggest that joining hands in prayer is one of the most important things we can do for each other. Point out prayer as one of the ways of serving identified on the cross banner. Open your time with a prayer:

"Loving God, thank you for creating us as people with many gifts. Help us discover the ways that we can use these gifts to share with people in need. Bless our time together and help each one of us to develop the strong heart of a servant. Amen."

Sing a familiar song about reaching out to others with God's love, such as "Love, Love, Love, That's What It's All About."

Dramatize the story of The Good Samaritan by asking volunteers to pantomime the various roles as you or a volunteer reads the story aloud from Luke 10: 25-37. Encourage some audience participation by suggesting they compliment the Good Samaritan after each good deed he does by cheering, "Go, Sam, Go!"

After the story, remind the participants that this passage is called the story of the Good Samaritan. Ask, "What makes the Good Samaritan good?" Acknowledge each response. Comment on the story, using these talking points:

■ Jesus told this story to help us understand that God expects us to love God and others.

■ Jesus referred to other people, without exception, as our neighbors. His story points out that being a neighbor crosses ethnic and racial lines.

■ In Jesus' time, Samaritans and Jews feared and hated each other. When this parable was told, many listeners probably thought that the person who was in the ditch should be the Samaritan. Then the priest and the Levite would have had a good excuse to pass him by. Instead it is the Jew who is in the ditch and it is the hated Samaritan who stops to care for him. The Samaritan does not ask his race or religion, he knows it and bears the Jew in his arms anyway. What counts here is caring for a fellow human being, a child of God who is in need.

Ask the participants to review the various ways in which the good Samaritan served the needs of a man who was hurting. Invite them to associate each deed with a way of serving identified on the cross banner. (Luke 10:34—active service or "Do." Luke 20:35—advocacy or "Speak" and giving of one's resources or "Give.")

Comment, "Jesus modeled this same compassion, concern, and love for those he encountered. Because of the grace, mercy, and love that God shows us each day, we are compelled to do as Jesus did and look at the needs of others with a servant heart! Jesus modeled the greatest act of service when he expressed his total love for us by paying the price for our sins on the cross. He asks us to devote our lives to nurturing a cross-shaped relationship between God and other people." (Draw a vertical line and talk about our relationship with God as vertical. Draw a horizontal line over the vertical line and talk about God's desire for us to reach out to others.) Also note that regular opportunities to serve are an important part of the healthy development of children and youth.

Close your opening with another song from your hymnal or songbook about caring for others, such as "They'll Know We Are Christians By Our Love."

ASSET 9, Service to Others. Young person serves in the community one hour or more per week. Outdoor ministry sites and congregations build this asset by teaching about faith-based servanthood and by providing intergenerational and age-specific opportunities for serving in the congregation, outdoor ministry site, and community.

MAKING FAITH CONNECTIONS

Gifted to serve (25 minutes)

Purpose: To help participants assess their own gifts and interests for service.

Introduce the concept of gifts or passions for service as similar to the special abilities and talents God gives each of us to be athletes, musicians, leaders, writers, builders, and so on. We are gifted to serve others in specific ways. Refer to the ways of serving identified on the cross banner as you describe these four ways to serve, using these talking points:

■ **Do**

For some, hands-on work is the most satisfying way to serve. Clearing a nature trail, building with Habitat for Humanity, cooking in a soup kitchen, and helping with chores at home are expressions of a person's need to dig in and get their hands dirty.

■ **Speak**

Others are gifted in the way that they are able to speak up for others. These advocates write letters, make phone calls, and talk to their neighbors to raise awareness of issues and speak out against injustice.

■ **Pray**

Some people, who understand deeply that God is at the center of all we do, are faithful and diligent in their prayers for those in need and the people who serve to meet those needs.

■ **Give**

Another way that people respond to Jesus' call to "go and do likewise" is by giving of their money and other resources, knowing that their earthly goods are blessings to share.

Comment that these four ways of serving are equally valuable and necessary. Distribute copies of the Gifted to Serve reproducible sheet and pencils. Direct participants to form teams of four to six people. Make sure that each team includes more than one generation, but be sensitive to family units who want to remain together.

Allow about ten minutes for participants to individually complete the survey. Encourage adults and children to work together as needed to clarify questions and tally their responses. As participants finish, invite them to take one of their hand-print name tags and tape them to the cross banner, placing them in the area of the cross that is the same as their strongest way of serving.

Ask team members to discuss these questions among themselves:

■ In which way of serving are you the strongest?
■ Which way of serving could use strengthening in your life?
■ Tell about your most meaningful experience serving others.

Invite them to encourage one another by suggesting practical and age appropriate ways they each might use their gifts for service.

Break (10 minutes)

Serve a snack of your choice and encourage participants to mingle and get to know each other better.

Service station activities (35 minutes)

Purpose: To explore more deeply the different ways of serving.

Introduce the Service Stations as places where

participants explore the four ways of serving. Tell participants that they will have time to visit two stations. Suggest that they visit the stations that are the same as their two top ways of serving from the Gifted to Serve sheet, but give them the option of exploring the others. Orient participants to the locations of the stations and introduce the attendants at each one. Arrange a signal such as a bell or horn that will sound after 15 minutes to tell participants it's time to change stations.

Service station idea starters

(Customize the activities in each station to fit the needs of your outdoor ministry site, congregation, or community.)

Do Station idea starters

- Assemble hygiene kits for a homeless shelter. Check with local shelter for needed items, such as toothbrushes, combs, shampoo, deodorant, etc.
- Pick up trash around the outdoor ministry site or neighborhood grounds.
- Sort and pack clothing and food donations for a local clothing cupboard or food pantry.
- Assemble a mailing for your outdoor ministry site or congregation.
- Other ideas of activities for your location...

Give Station idea starters

- "Months and Months of Giving." Draw 12 squares on a piece of chart paper and label with the months of the year. Ask participants to add ideas for giving for each month of the calendar year. For example, in January, celebrate the New Year by bringing dimes for a special offering, one per year of age. December's giving might be mittens for the mitten tree. Give this chart to committee leaders and planners for their use.
- Check out a new resource, "Open a World of Possibility: Creating Traditions." Contact the ELCA World Hunger Appeal (800) 638-3522 to request copies. Choose one or two activities to consider.
- Set up a computer and explore web sites of popular charities. Ask: "How can we learn if our money is going to be used wisely?"

- Other ideas of activities for your location...

Pray Station idea starters

- Prayer Chain. Cut strips of copier paper into 1 1/2" x 4" lengths. Ask participants to write a social issue or personal concern needing prayer on each one. Gather in a circle to offer a prayer for what is mentioned on each slip of paper, assembling the chain with a glue stick as your prayer goes around the circle. Take the chain to closing worship. After the event, check with your congregation about the possibility of including the concern from one link each Sunday in the prayers of the church or the bulletin. A list of prayer concerns could also be put in the newsletter for your outdoor ministry site.
- Great Cloud of Witnesses. On a sheet of poster board, draw one large cloud. Ask participants to write in the cloud the names of individuals they know and admire who have a strong servant heart. It could be a fellow congregation member or someone in the community. Offer a prayer of thanksgiving for these servants.
- Mount a tablet of plain paper on a piece of poster board that is slightly larger. Decorate this with markers and label it, "My Prayer List." Participants can take these home and keep them in a handy place to jot down reminders of prayer requests.
- Other ideas of activities for your location...

Speak Station idea starters

- Provide paper, pens, and stamps for participants to use to write a letter to a government official about a topic that concerns them. Be sure to have a chart of names of your local officials and their addresses.
- Create awareness posters using markers and pictures and words cut from magazines to address an issue of the individual's choice (for example, encouraging others to volunteer, the importance of staying in school, the need to resolve conflict peacefully). These posters can be taken to participant's congregation, work, school, or community center and posted there as an educational tool and conversation starter.

- Check out "The Giving Market: An ELCA Children's Hunger Program" or "The Real Meal Deal: A Youth Hunger Justice Retreat" for other advocacy ideas for children and youth. Contact the ELCA World Hunger Appeal at (800) 638-3522 to request a copy.
- Other ideas of activities for your location...

■ "Send Me" towels
(15 minutes)

Purpose: To create a symbol of Christian service to use during worship and to take home.

Introduce this activity by reading aloud John 13:5, 12-15:

He put some water into a large bowl: Then he began washing his disciples' feet and drying them with the towel he was wearing...After Jesus had washed his disciples' feet and had put his outer garment back on, he sat down again. Then he said: "Do you understand what I have done? You call me your teacher and Lord, and you should, because that is who I am. And if your Lord and teacher has washed your feet, you should do the same for each other. I have set the example, and you should do for each other exactly what I have done for you."

Comment that foot washing was a common task of hospitality in Bible times because most people wore sandals or went bare foot. Because Jesus washed the feet of his disciples, the towel is a symbol of Christian compassion.

Invite each participant to decorate a towel with symbols and phrases reflecting the heart of a servant. (For example, "Use Me, O Lord," "Here I Am, Send Me," "Go and Do Likewise," "Love Your Neighbor.") Add rubber stamps in the shape of a hand, a foot, a cross, or a heart; fabric scraps cut in these shapes; or simple drawings to complete the design. Suggest that, unless there are personal feelings of attachment to the towels they designed, the towels will be placed on the altar and exchanged with someone else in the group to encourage them to grow as a servant.

Closing (10 minutes)

Arrange the "Send Me" Towels around the altar. Gather volunteers and the supplies for the foot-washing if you choose to do this activity during the reading from John 13.

Begin your closing by singing a few songs about serving from a familiar songbook or hymnal.

Ask a volunteer to read aloud John 13:5-15. During the presentation, volunteers may demonstrate the act of footwashing.

Next, call each person forward to receive a "Send Me" towel and recognize them as servants in Jesus' name. When all towels are distributed, lead participants in a litany of commitment. Ask the participants to respond to each petition with the words of the prophet Isaiah, "Here I am. Send me."

Litany

Leader: Lord, we know of many people who are sad and lonely. Who will extend mercy, kindness, and compassion to them?

Group: Here I am. Send Me!

Leader: God of all creation, we forget how fragile our lakes, rivers, forests, and prairies are. Who will make sure that these gifts to us remain clean and cared for?

Group: Here I am. Send Me!

Leader: Lord, we live in abundance, yet in too many places across our community and throughout the world, children die from hunger, malnutrition and disease. Who will share generously of their money, time, and goods?

Group: Here I am. Send Me!

Leader: Lord, the world is full of injustice and inhumanity. Many of our sisters and brothers are not able to speak up for themselves or are not heard. Who will be a voice for the disabled, the persecuted, the forgotten, or the mistreated?

Group: Here I am. Send Me!

Leader: Gracious God, you have gifted us, each in a different way to walk and talk and act as Jesus did. Who will serve, give, pray, and speak for your children in need?

Group: Here I am. Send Me!

GIFTED TO SERVE

This simple tool is designed to help you identify the ways in which God has gifted you to serve. Read each statement and circle the appropriate response according to this code:

1=never 2=sometimes 3=rarely 4=frequently

Do

	4 3 2 1
I work in a soup kitchen or other community service agency.	4 3 2 1
I help neighbors with their chores.	4 3 2 1
I work on clean-up day projects at my congregation or outdoor ministry site.	4 3 2 1
I go on mission trips—visiting special places to help others.	4 3 2 1
I am not bothered by the hard work, long hours, or dirty conditions often encountered at a disaster site.	4 3 2 1
I feel satisfied when I have spent many hours repeatedly doing the same thing such as packing clothes, stuffing envelopes, or raking yards.	4 3 2 1
I like to see immediate results from my work such as a freshly painted fence, a weeded community garden, or a smile on the face of a shut-in.	4 3 2 1

Give

I like to respond when the church asks for donations (canned goods, mittens, school supplies, clothing, etc.).	4 3 2 1
I ask for pledges for myself or else sponsor someone in a fund-raising activity such as Crop Walk, bike-a-thon, etc.	4 3 2 1
I send money or give special offerings when I learn of a disaster in another community or an individual in a life-threatening situation.	4 3 2 1
I respond to service opportunities that do not require me to leave my home—activities where my primary contribution is my time.	4 3 2 1
I give money or goods anonymously when I learn of a need in the congregation or community.	4 3 2 1

Pray

I pray for the victims, as well as the caregivers, when I hear of a tragedy in the news.	4 3 2 1
I urge others to pray about an illness or a specific social issue, injustice, or personal challenge.	4 3 2 1
I keep a prayer list in a prominent place so I can be reminded daily of prayer needs.	4 3 2 1
I send notes or email messages to encourage people who are hurting and let them know I am praying for them.	4 3 2 1
I pray for myself, asking God to give me the understanding, wisdom, courage, strength, or sensitivity to care for people who are different from me.	4 3 2 1

Speak

I am the first person to speak up about an issue or to support an individual in need.	4 3 2 1
I participate in public rallies to show support for a cause that is important to me.	4 3 2 1
I enjoy listening to the news, engaging in conversations, or reading magazines to learn more about social issues.	4 3 2 1
I write letters of protest or advocacy to government officials.	4 3 2 1
I sign petitions for issues that are important to me.	4 3 2 1
I participate in Bible studies or other kinds of discussion groups that explore root causes of injustice.	4 3 2 1

When you have completed all the questions, look at the number of 4's you circled. In which area did you circle the most? Put a star beside that way of serving—it is your strongest gift for serving others.

Now look at the number of 1's you circled. In which area did you circle the most? Put an arrow beside that way of serving—it is a way of serving that you may want to investigate.

In some cases, your responses may be equal or close in all categories. That just means that you have experience in many types of serving.

STOPS, STARTS, AND CRUISE ON THROUGH

EXPLORE BOUNDARIES AND ROLES

This intergenerational event links:

- The skills of setting and honoring personal boundaries;
- The faith practice of encouragement; and
- Asset 11, Family Boundaries.

KEY LEARNING POINTS

✔ What we value about ourselves and our relationships with others helps us define our boundaries.

✔ Each child of God has a right to be treated with love and respect and has the privilege or responsibility of returning the favor to others.

✔ We encourage one another through word and deed to understand our lives as God's children.

KEY BIBLE TEXTS

Children, you show love for others by truly helping them, and not merely by talking about it.

1 John 3:18

BACKGROUND FOR THE LEADER

Jesus taught people about the dynamics of faith and community. He helped people claim the joy of being in a relationship with God, then went on to teach them definite boundaries and expectations for relating to others as God's people. Personal identities are shaped within the context of community. Our involvement in and commitment to a relationship with Jesus helps us appreciate our individual gifts and abilities for enriching the body of Christ. As we discover the depth and strength of our iden-

tity in Christ, we are empowered to nurture relationships that reflect the same integrity.

During this event, participants will discover the significance of their individual roles and identities and consider some of the boundaries necessary for living in a healthy community. Asset 11, Family Boundaries, points out the importance that these clear rules and consequences have in the healthy development of young lives. Within the family of faith, we encourage one another in word and deed to consider appropriate roles and boundaries for children of God of all ages.

EVENT SCHEDULE

Let's gather		
If I were a car	20	minutes
Making faith connections		
There's no place like home	15	minutes
Quick starts	20	minutes
Heart kites	10	minutes
Break	10	minutes
C.O.G. alert	10	minutes
Heart Starts game	30	minutes
Closing	5	minutes

MATERIALS NEEDED

If I were a car

- If I Were A Car reproducible sheet from page 52
- Pencils

There's no place like home

- One sheet of construction paper in a light color for each household
- Markers

Quick starts
- Chart paper, markers
- Quick Starts reproducible sheet from page 53

Heart kites
- Red construction paper, one 9" x 12" piece per person
- Paper punch, scissors
- Yarn, 24" per person
- Cardboard patterns: 3" heart and 9" circle

Break
- Snack mix ingredients as you choose: assorted cereals, small candies, raisins, nuts, etc.
- Serving bowls and spoons
- Small paper cups, one per person

C.O.G. alert
- Chart paper, markers
- Bibles
- Water in a bowl

Heart Starts game
- Heart Puzzle reproducible sheet on page 54
- Markers, scissors

PREPARATION

- Tend to the ministry of hospitality by providing name tags and making sure that there is comfortable seating for all participants.
- Make a copy of the If I Were A Car reproducible sheet for each person.
- Have a circle of chairs for the If I Were A Car game. Each person needs a chair.
- Make one copy of the Quick Starts reproducible sheet for each team of six persons. Cut the cards on each sheet apart and paper clip as a set.
- On a sheet of chart paper, copy these phrases:
  - **L** = Let yourself love and be loved, forgive and be forgiven.
  - **O** = Own your own thoughts, emotions, and behaviors; let others do the same.
  - **V** = Value the gifts, personalities, and perspectives of each person; respect their right to share them.
  - **E** = Embrace one another daily; encourage each other to grow as individuals.

- Make a Heart Kite as a sample, following directions on page 49.
- On a piece of chart paper, copy the illustration of the baby in the baptismal font from page 50. If you prefer, you could also trace this on an overhead transparency and use a projector.
- Mark each of these verses in a separate Bible so that volunteer readers can find them quickly: Ephesians 5:1; John 15:12; Matthew 5: 14-16; 1 Thessalonians 5:11; Romans 12:9-12.
- Make a copy of the Heart Puzzle reproducible sheet for each person.

> Throughout this session, small groups are called teams to differentiate them from the large group. Whenever you see the term *group*, it refers to all the teams together.

LET'S GATHER

If I were a car (20 minutes)

Purpose: To become more aware of the variety of participants gathered.

Greet people as they arrive. Give each one "If I Were A Car" sheet to complete while other participants are arriving. Encourage youth to help younger children with the reading.

When most have finished the sheet, begin by associating this activity with the title of this program. Suggest that before we go anywhere, we need to choose the "cars" we feel most comfortable "driving" through this event. Read each of the car types in the first question and ask for a show of hands of people who choose to identify with each one. Comment on how the variety of interests, gifts, and talents of the participants gathered is even more rich than the variety of cars in the parking lot.

Have the participants take their sheets to the circle of chairs and find a place to "park." Invite them to introduce themselves to each other, telling why they chose the type of car they did.

Next, play a game of Bumper Cars (played like Fruit Basket Upset).

Directions for Bumper Cars:

1. Be sure there are only as many chairs in the circle as there are people. The leader should not have a chair. The leader stands in the center of the circle and calls out a specific speed, parking place, level of gasoline, etc. from the "If I Were A Car" activity sheet. Participants who have chosen that option get up and quickly switch "parking" places with someone else who's on the move. During this time, the leader rejoins the group by taking one of the empty chairs.

2. The person left without a chair becomes the next leader and calls out another item. Participants switch places as before. Periodically, leaders may opt to just say "Bumper Cars." At this signal, everyone switches places.

3. Continue the game until everyone has had the opportunity to switch seats a few times.

Comment: "Our lives are sometimes like this game. There are days when we encounter obstacles and confusing or embarrassing moments when we express our opinions or try to figure out which way to go. Sometimes we step on each others' toes or act without thinking about how our actions are affecting someone else."

Ask the group to join you in prayer: "Loving God, you have created each one of us as your unique and precious child. Be with us today and help us discover ways to encourage each other to live in your family in healthy and loving ways. Amen."

MAKING FAITH CONNECTIONS

There's no place like home! (15 minutes)

Purpose: To consider the roles of individual family members and some of the ways they influence each other's lives.

Ask participants to sit with other members of their households. Give each household a sheet of construction paper and some markers. Invite participants who are single to gather in a group and work side-by-side as they identify family and friends who may be present in heart and mind, but reside outside their homes.

Have each household fold the paper in half and draw a picture of their home on the outside. On the inside, have them draw the outline of a heart. Invite them to work together to draw a family snapshot—pictures of all the children, youth, and adults who make up their immediate family. Family members that live in the same household should be drawn inside the illustration of their home. The people whom they consider "immediate" family but who do not live in the same home should be drawn inside the heart. As they list family members, tell them to make note of the various roles each person plays—daughter, step-brother, grandpa, etc.—in addition to her or his name.

When they have completed this exercise, invite them to make a team with the participants sitting closest to them. Within the teams, participants should introduce themselves, telling where their homes are located, as well as giving a quick introduction to the individual family members in their drawings.

Then ask the small teams to discuss these questions: How do people inside your home affect each other? How do the people you drew inside the heart influence the lives of the people you drew inside the home?

To the large group, comment on how our relationships with other people in our family influence the role that we play.

> **ASSET 11, Family Boundaries. Family has clear rules and consequences, and monitors the young person's whereabouts. In your ministry, you build this asset by communicating the importance of roles, boundaries, expectations, and accountability in family life in the home as well as life within God's family.**

Quick starts (20 minutes)

Purpose: To explore how our perspectives of one another shape our relationships.

Divide the large group into teams of six to eight persons. Encourage family units to stay together if they like. Introduce this activity as an opportunity to get to know each other better.

Give each team one packet of the Quick Starts cards you prepared from the reproducible sheet. Appoint the person wearing the longest shoe as the team leader. The team leader draws one card from the pack and reads it aloud. Each person on the team then takes a turn responding, though remind participants that it is always OK to say, "pass." The leader continues to draw and read cards until all have been used.

After teams have completed responding to the cards, call them back to the large group.

Ask these questions, inviting a few volunteers to respond to each one.

1. Were you surprised by some of the answers? Why or why not?

2. If you're here with members of your household, how do you feel about the responses given by them? Does it bother you? Intrigue you or delight you? How do you feel about the responses given by other members of the family of God?

3. What insights did this activity offer you into some of the agreements or disagreements you may have in your household or in our congregational family?

Comment: "The individual choices that were made reflect the different ways we are 'wired'—some people are more playful or imaginative, some are more organized or analytical. Every family is made up of unique individuals, and that's true for God's family in this group, too. The more information we share with each other, the better able we are to understand each other's personalities. This leads to stronger relationships. Sometimes we discover things about each other that conflict with our ideas and perspectives and we are faced with the challenge of how we should respond. That's when we need to remember that our motivation to love one another is not our own."

Highlight the words of 1 John 4 :19, "We love because God first loved us" as you celebrate the fact that it's God love for us that motivates us to love one

another. Clarify that loving someone doesn't just mean saying that we love them. Refer to 1 John 3:18, "Children, you show love for others by truly helping them, and not merely by talking about it." Display the L.O.V.E. chart as you further explain this verse.

L = Let yourself love and be loved, forgive and be forgiven as you reflect God's love and grace.

O = Own your own thoughts, emotions, and behaviors, and expect others to do the same.

V = Value the gifts, personalities, and perspectives of each person; respect their right to share them.

E = Embrace one another in daily community and encourage each other to grow as individuals.

Say, "Part of the healthy development of young people in our families and in our congregation is helping them to set appropriate boundaries, rules, and expectations based on this L.O.V.E. and to lovingly encourage them to honor these for themselves and for others in the family."

Spend a few minutes encouraging group members to name some of the rules and expectations that people of all ages could follow in their everyday lives to reflect this L.O.V.E. (Some responses might include: No put-downs in our language; taking an interest in each other's daily activities; using "I" language when expressing feelings or opinions; respecting each other's need for community time and individual time, etc.)

Heart Kites (10 minutes)
Purpose: To create a playful reminder of God's love for our families.

Set out the paper, patterns, scissors, paper punch, pencils, and yarn on a resource table. Show the Heart Kite you made as a sample as you give the instructions:

1. On the construction paper, trace the heart pattern in the center. Around it trace the circle pattern.
2. Begin by cutting out the circle. Then cut in a spiral toward the heart. When you reach the heart, cut around it, but make sure to leave it connected to the spiral.
3. Punch a hole in the heart and tie a piece of yarn through it.
4. Fly the kite by running with the kite string held in a hand outstretched behind you.

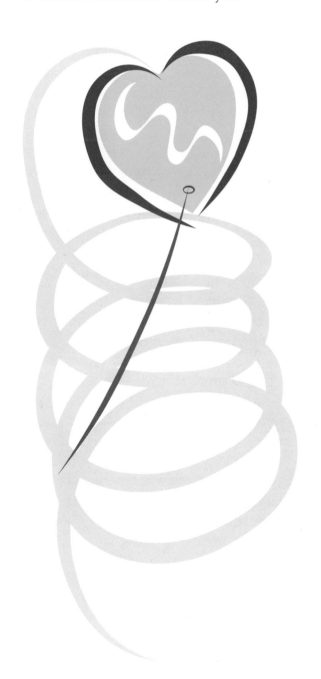

Break (10 minutes)

Enlist some volunteers to help mix this snack. Use spoons to scoop it into small paper cups for serving. Or, you may choose to set out bowls of each ingredient and let participants mix their own in their cups.

C.O.G. alert (10 minutes)

Purpose: To consider and celebrate our identity and responsibilities as children of God.

Begin by pointing out the drawing of the baby in the baptismal font on the chart paper or transparency. Remind the group that Baptism is God's love and grace given to us, making us God's children. As we are marked with the cross of Christ, we are identified as a member of God's own family for eternity. If you are comfortable with the practice, invite participants to dip their fingers in the bowl of water and mark the sign of the cross on their foreheads to commemorate their baptisms.

Say, "We are special people—C.O.G.s—Children of God! As God's special people, we have a special calling. It's really quite a job description." Give the marked Bibles to volunteers who are willing to read aloud. After each verse is read, invite the group to give some examples of what they might do each day to live out this calling.

Do as God does. After all, you are his dear children.

Ephesians 5:1

Now I tell you to love each other, as I have loved you.

John 15:12

You are like light for the whole world. A city built on top of a hill cannot be hidden, and no one would light a lamp and put it under a clay pot. A lamp is placed on a lamp stand, where it can give light to everyone in the house. Make your light shine, so that others will see the good that you do and will praise your Father in heaven.

Matthew 5:14-16

That's why you must encourage and help each other, just as you are already doing.

1 Thessalonians 5:11

Be sincere in your love for others. Hate everything that is evil and hold tight to everything that is good. Love each other as brothers and sisters and honor others more than you do yourself. Never give up. Eagerly follow the Holy Spirit and serve the Lord. Let your hope make you glad. Be patient in time of trouble and never stop praying.

Romans 12:9-12

Heart Starts game (30 minutes)

Purpose: To grow in understanding about how to set and honor boundaries in loving ways.

First, ask each person to cut out four cars from the "If I Were A Car" sheet used earlier. Then give each person a copy of the "Heart Puzzle" reproducible sheet from page 54. Encourage them to color the sheets as desired as you use these talking points for an introduction to the activity:

■ Ask the group to name different ways they have learned what love is.

■ Point out the phrases on the heart puzzle and read aloud 1 Corinthians 13:4-8

Love is kind and patient,
never jealous, boastful, proud, or rude.
Love isn't selfish or quick tempered.
It doesn't keep a record of wrongs that others do.
Love rejoices in the truth, but not in evil.
Love is always supportive, loyal, hopeful, and trusting.
Love never fails!

■ Loving other people is really about honoring them as the unique individuals God has created them to be. It is also about honoring our own lives as we nurture the relationships we have with them.

■ Sometimes disappointing and challenging things happen in our lives. These times threaten to overwhelm us and tempt us to stop doing the very things we need to do to help us through it. Sometimes we just need to stop and think again about what to do to take care of our needs by setting our own rules and boundaries, and also to honor the needs, rules, and boundaries of others.

■ This game is called "Stops, Starts, and Cruise On Through." It will help us think about honoring our own needs and the needs of others.

Divide the group into teams of six to eight persons. Make sure each team is intergenerational. Encourage children who are not comfortable reading to play with an older buddy. Explain the directions. As you play the first round, repeat the directions step-by-step:

1. Read aloud one of the stories below.

2. As participants listen to the story, they should look on their game boards to find the phrases about love that they think connect to the story. They can place a car on each puzzle piece that they think applies.

3. Within the small teams, participants should compare notes about where they placed their cars.

4. Ask small teams to then discuss which actions (if any) they think that people in the story should stop, what actions (if any) they think the people in the story could start, and which actions (if any) they think the people in the story should continue or, in other words, "cruise on through."

Heart Start stories

A father and his daughter went to pick up her older brother at school. When the brother approached the car and saw that his sister was sitting in the front seat, he demanded that she get in the back immediately.

A little boy had a grandma who lived far away. When he was getting ready to go on an airplane to visit his grandma, his parents told him he could only bring along one toy. When he got to his grandma's, he was surprised to see that Grandma had stocked a "While You Stay" play box with some special toys just for him. She plans to get it out every time he comes.

Your cousins call to tell you all about the new equipment they got for their family room—a 60" television, a foosball table, and a full stock of exercise equipment. They make a point of telling you how much all of it cost and how hard they worked to impress their bosses to get the great salary increases to pay for it all "in cash!" Your cousins say that they can only imagine how tough it must be to crowd around your 19" television.

A 15-year-old girl made plans to join her friends at the mall without asking permission. She then discovered that her mom had other plans and could not provide the needed transportation. The daughter yelled at her mom, insisting that she delay her plans and drive her to meet her friends.

Two brothers, Tom and Jerry, wanted the same video game. For Christmas, Tom got the game as a gift from his uncle, but Jerry got a different game. Jerry tried to make a trade, but Tom was not interested. Finally, Jerry shouted, "Fine! I don't care! I don't like your game anyway!"

An older sister was helping her younger brother with his math homework. He was having a hard time, but she showed him how to do it, step-by-step, and gave fun examples to ease the stress and help him understand.

As you wind up these games, encourage participants to take their game boards home and to try this process using experiences that they have each day. This can encourage family members of all ages to consider their own needs and the needs of others in loving ways.

Summarize the key learning points of this session before you move into the closing.

- What we value about ourselves and our relationships with others help us define our boundaries.
- Each child of God has a right to be treated with love and respect and has the privilege or responsibility of returning the favor to others.
- We encourage one another through word and deed to understand our lives as God's children.

Closing (5 minutes)

End your time together by gathering participants into a circle and asking them to join in the following cheer with you.

Leader: Give me an "L"

Group: "L"

Leader: Give me an "O"

Group: "O"

Leader: Giver me a "V"

Group: "V"

Leader: Give me an "E"

Group: "E"

Leader: What does it spell?

Group: Love!

Leader: And what does love make us want to do? Repeat after me—Stop! Start or Cruise on Through! We've got to think it through!

G: Stop! Start or Cruise on Through? We've got to think it through!

L: And, no matter what, we're going to make sure God's love is flowing through. Right?

G: Right!

L: Amen! Go in peace and serve the Lord!

G: Thanks be to God!

IF I WERE A CAR

1. If I were a car today, I'd like to be a:
- Shiny sports car
- Old pick-up truck
- Sport utility vehicle
- A small sedan

2. If I were a car today, my favorite speed would be:
- 20 mph
- 45 mph
- 60 mph
- 90 mph

3. If I were a car today, my gas tank would read:
- Almost empty
- Half full
- Filled to the top

4. If I were a car today, I would be most proud of:
- My radio (my ability to entertain or communicate)
- My headlights (my ability to see things through)
- My tires (my gifts and abilities)
- My upholstery (my appearance)

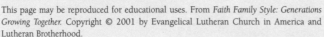
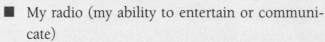
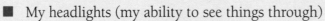
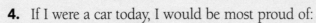

Quick Start

When making plans to do something with a group of friends, I usually:

a. am the one with all the ideas

b. enjoy coordinating all the details

c. try hard to get my own way

d. am comfortable with whatever the group decides—I just kind of "go along for the ride"

Quick Start

When I go to a beach I usually:

a. go out and splash in the waves

b. stand or sit and look out at the water and sky

c. keep my nose to the ground looking for shells or stones

d. go for a brisk walk along the edge of the water

Quick Start

I usually think about buying gas for the car when:

a. I see a sign for real cheap gas

b. the warning light comes on

c. it's Saturday—I always buy on the same day every week

d. the gas gauge reads 1/4 full

Quick Start

After I go to see a movie, I am most likely to remember:

a. the music, actors' names, and locations

b. the story line and the personality of the characters

c. not much, because I napped through most of it

d. the special effects, lighting, and sound effects

Quick Start

When I was five and made a mistake on a school paper I would:

a. erase it carefully and make corrections

b. scribble over them and continue

c. crumple up my paper and start all over again

d. go do something else

Quick Start

When I hear about a new book that sounds interesting, I usually:

a. wait to see if it'll come out in a movie

b. look for an audio tape to listen to it

c. read it

d. ask someone else who has read it to tell me about it

Quick Start

When I'm having company over for dinner, I usually:

a. spend so much time planning what we'll do after dinner that I almost forget to think about what we're going to eat

b. plan a meal that turns into a major project

c. ask the guests to bring part of the meal

d. order pizza or carry out

Quick Start

When I get a phone call, I usually:

a. concentrate on the conversation

b. pace the floor or walk around the house while I talk

c. watch TV out of the corner of my eye

d. can't wait to hang up

Heart Starts

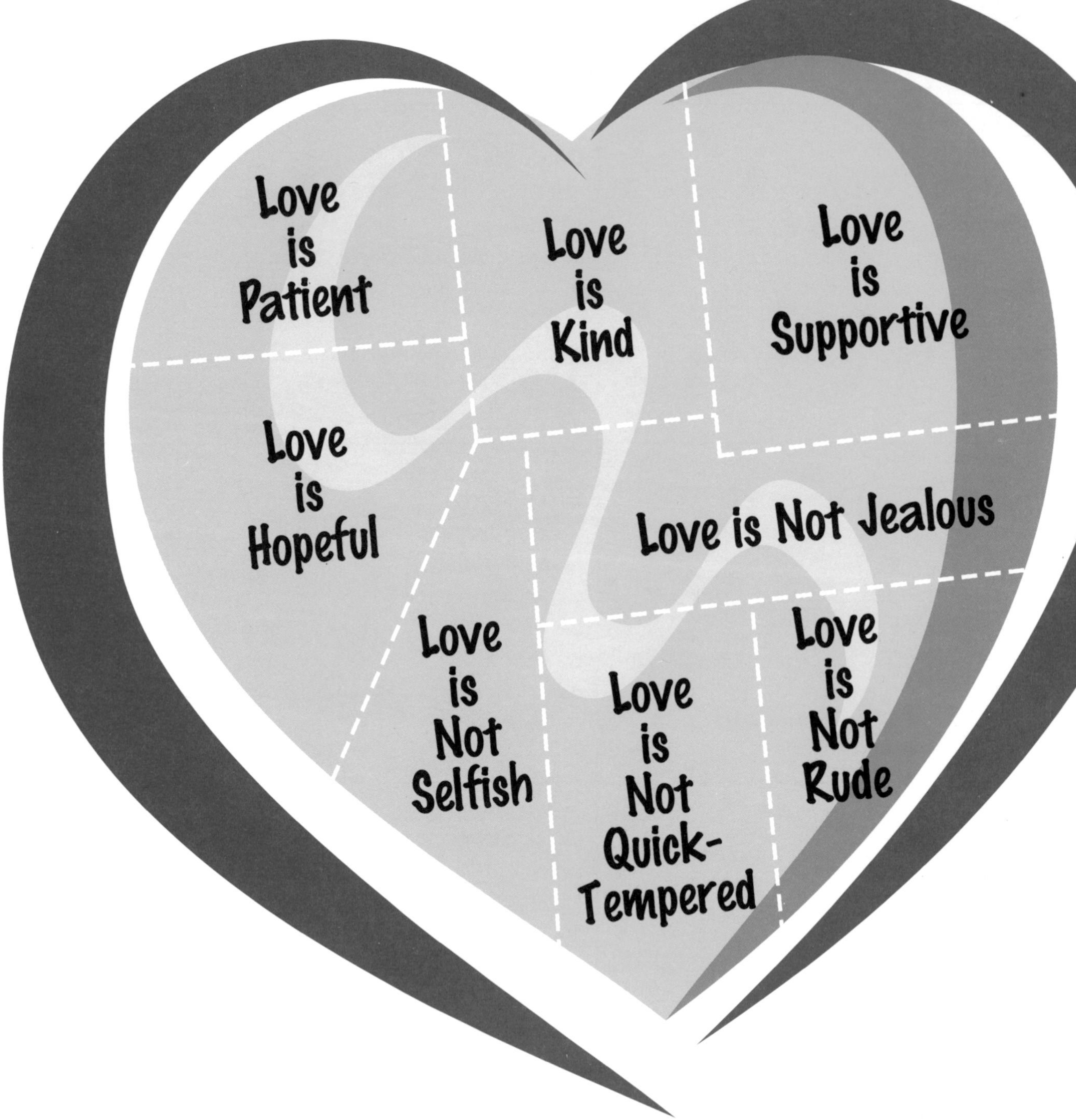

Love
is
Patient

Love
is
Kind

Love
is
Supportive

Love
is
Hopeful

Love is Not Jealous

Love
is
Not
Selfish

Love
is
Not
Quick-
Tempered

Love
is
Not
Rude

WORKIN' IT THRU

WORK THROUGH CONFLICT WITH LOVE AND FORGIVENESS

THIS INTERGENERATIONAL EVENT LINKS:

- The skills for positive conflict resolution;
- The faith practice of prayer; and
- Asset 36, Peaceful Conflict Resolution.

KEY LEARNING POINTS

✔ Conflict is a normal part of healthy relationships.
✔ We can encounter and work through conflict in positive ways.
✔ Forgiveness is a gift that God gives us and we, in turn, give to others.

KEY BIBLE TEXTS

If one of my followers sins against you, go and point out what was wrong. But do it in private, just between the two of you. If that person listens, you have won back a follower. But if that one refuses to listen, take along one or two others.

Matthew 18: 15-16a

BACKGROUND FOR THE LEADER

In the course of all relationships, there are times of conflict, ranging from major and life-changing ("Where will we live?") to the trivial ("Whose turn is it to run the remote?"). Conflicts, arguments, and disagreements are normal between people who think, act, and believe differently. Though most people recognize this, it is still easy to be taken by surprise at conflict and to respond in ways that do not help our relationships to grow stronger. This event is planned to help individuals practice ways to respond to conflict in healthy ways.

The ability to respond to conflict in peaceful and life-giving ways is a key building block in the development of children and youth, and a cornerstone skill for adults. During this event, participants

EVENT SCHEDULE

Let's gather
What shape are you in?	**20 minutes**

Making faith connections
Red Light, Green Light	**10 minutes**
S.T.O.P.	**20 minutes**
Stoplight door hanger	**10 minutes**
Break	**10 minutes**
S.T.O.P. practice	**10 minutes**
Prayer table tent	**10 minutes**

Closing
Confession and forgiveness	**15 minutes**

will experience how this skill can be strengthened by the practice of prayer.

MATERIALS NEEDED

What shape are you in?

- Index cards, one per person
- Safety pins, one per person
- l" round stickers in red, yellow, and green; one of each color for each person
- Markers

- Chenille stems (pipe cleaners) in four different colors; plan to have an equal number of stems in each color; each person will get one chenille stem

Red Light, Green Light
- One sheet of red paper
- One sheet of green paper

S.T.O.P.
- Chart paper
- Red, yellow, and green markers

Stoplight hangers
- Stoplight reproducible sheet on page 60
- Scissors, markers
- Staplers or transparent tape

Break
- Six vanilla wafer cookies per person
- Small bowls of red, yellow, and green icing
- Knives for spreading icing
- One paper plate for each person
- Ice water or other beverage

S.T.O.P. practice
- S.T.O.P. Cards reproducible sheet on page 61

Prayer table tent
- Fresh Start Prayer reproducible sheet on page 62
- 9"x12" construction paper, one sheet per person
- Scissors
- Staplers or white glue

Confession and forgiveness
- Worship books

PREPARATION

- On a sheet of chart paper, draw the outlines of three large circles, stacked like a traffic light. Do not color in the circles.
- Make copies of the Stoplight reproducible sheet on page 60, one for each participant. Make a sample Stoplight Hanger.
- Make copies of the S.T.O.P. Cards reproducible sheet on page 61. Make one copy for each team of six persons. Cut each sheet apart and put the cards into a packet with a paperclip.
- Make copies of the Fresh Start Prayer reproducible sheet on page 62, one for each participant. Make a sample Prayer Table Tent.

LET'S GATHER

What shape are you in? (20 minutes)

Purpose: To learn each other's names and begin to consider the theme of the day.

As participants gather, invite them to make traffic light name tags by placing a green, yellow, and red dot along one edge of an index card to resemble a traffic light. Ask them to write their names on the cards with markers and use safety pins to wear them.

> Throughout this session, small groups are called teams to differentiate them from the large group. Whenever you see the term group, it refers to all the teams together.

Welcome the group. Give each person a chenille stem. Ask them to bend it into a shape that tells how they are feeling as they begin this event today. After they have done this, have participants form teams of four persons, with each team having each of the colors of chenille stems represented. (Be sensitive to family units who want to stay together—encourage them to trade colors with others.)

In each small team, have members introduce themselves and tell about the shape they made. Next, ask participants to straighten out their chenille stems. Direct each person to bend it into a shape that shows what they think a perfect relationship should look like. Allow a few minutes for team members to share with each other about the shapes they make.

Comment, "We all have relationships with many other people. Not all are alike, but all have some things in common. During this event, we'll explore one of those things that all relationships have—conflict. And we'll also explore how to work through conflict in caring and positive ways that help people grow in healthy ways."

Pray, "Loving and forgiving God, you have created us to be in relationship with you and with the other people you have placed in our lives. Be with us during this time and open our hearts and minds to new ways of growing together in your grace and love. In the name of your Son, who taught us the most about your love and forgiveness, Amen."

MAKING FAITH CONNECTIONS

Red light, green light (10 minutes)

Purpose: To create an image to undergird the S.T.O.P. process of conflict resolution.

In a large open area, play a round or two of the children's playground game, "Red Light, Green Light." Directions for play:

1. Participants line up along a baseline at one end of the open area. The leader stands at the opposite end of the open area. The object of the game is to be the first person to tag the leader.

2. Participants move according to the signal given by the leader. When the leader holds up the green paper and calls out "green light," participants can begin walking toward the leader. When the leader holds up the red paper and calls out "Red light," participants must stop.

3. Participants who do not stop at the red paper signal must return to the baseline and start over.

4. The first person to tag the leader becomes the next leader.

> **Asset 36, Peaceful Conflict Resolution. Young person seeks to resolve conflict nonviolently. Outdoor ministry sites and congregations build this asset by providing opportunities for children and youth to learn and practice grace-filled ways to encounter and resolve conflict.**

S.T.O.P.

Purpose: To learn about a process to use to guide conflict resolution.

Gather the group. Comment on how well the participants understand red lights and green lights. Tell them they are ready to learn about a different kind of stoplight, the Stoplight approach to resolving conflict.

Use the chart paper you have prepared. Color in each circle as you tell about that color, using these talking points:

- Ask participants if they've ever said something they wish they wouldn't have, like called someone a name or spoken harshly. Point out that it's inevitable that we all do this because we're all human and we all sin and make mistakes.

- Ask them to name some of the things that have caused conflict between themselves and another person (such as misunderstanding, disagreements, not listening, nonverbal gestures, tone of voice). Comment that no matter how hard we try, we're going to make mistakes, and we are going to feel conflict with another person. The challenge is finding a positive and healthy way to respond to the conflicts that arise.

- A stoplight can help us remember a good process for dealing with conflict. Imagine that you're talking to a friend and you sense a conflict brewing. This moment is like approaching an intersection and seeing a YELLOW light. (Color the center circle yellow as you talk.)

- Ask the group to tell what a yellow light means in traffic. Then, tell how a yellow light in our process represents the signals that we sense that tell us we might need to stop and think about where we're headed and decide if we really want to go there. Do we want to speed up and cruise on through? Or should we stop? Ask the group to name some of the signals that might tell us we're at a yellow-light moment. (Raised voices, crying, whining, complaining, body language, refusing to speak, slamming a door, etc.)

- Say that a RED light can be a good thing at this point! (Color the top circle red. Then write the letters S, T, O, P as you explain.)

  S = Agree with the other person to take some time to step back and take a "snapshot" of the problem. During this break, figure out what the problem is—try to identify what is happening to cause the conflict. It is important to focus on WHAT the problem is, not WHO!

T = Take the time you need to cool off and think through what you'd like the end result to be.

O = Be open to talking with the other person about possible ways to resolve the conflict. Be ready to compromise and look at new ideas.

P = Proceed, remembering that your relationship with the other person is usually more important than the problem you're having at the moment.

■ (Color the bottom circle green.) When you're ready to continue in your relationship, go for it. Ask for forgiveness, accept the apology of the other, and begin to let go of the conflict. Be open to making a fresh new start.

■ There may be participants who have experienced situations where this type of process has not worked or could not work because of abuse or chemical dependency. Be sensitive to this, noting that this process is a guide for relationships where people are willing to work together in healthy ways to resolve the WHAT of their conflicts. In situations where one of the people involved is not committed to addressing the WHAT in healthy ways, help from other caring people like pastors, doctors, teachers, or counselors may be necessary. Jesus teaches us about this in Matthew, "If one of my followers sins against you, go and point out what was wrong. But do it in private, just between the two of you. If that person listens, you have won back a follower. But if that one refuses to listen, take along one or two others."

Stoplight hanger (10 minutes)

Purpose: To create a reminder of the S.T.O.P. process.

Show the sample and invite participants to make a stoplight door hanger to put on their refrigerator, bedroom door knob, bathroom mirror, or car dashboard. Distribute copies of the Stoplight repro-

ducible sheet and make markers, scissors, and staplers or tape available.

Break

Set out vanilla wafer cookies and the red, yellow, and green icing. Invite participants to make three sandwich cookies, one in each stoplight color. Encourage participants to get to know each other better as they snack.

S.T.O.P. practice

Purpose: To practice the S.T.O.P process.

Ask for two volunteers to come forward and read this vignette:

Brother: It's time to watch the news.

Sister: Oh, no you don't. It's my turn to choose and I choose the cartoon hour.

Brother: Give me that remote!

Sister: No way. The news is dumb and so are you!

Brother: Give it to me or I'll take it away from you!

Sister: You can't catch me!

Applaud the volunteers, then ask the participants to look at their Stoplight hangers. Say, "Clearly, these two need to stop and cool off. Let's walk them through this. First, "S"—what is the problem here? (Accept several responses. Make sure they focus on what, not who.) Now, "T"—if you were these two, what would you want the end result to be? What shape would you like your relationship to be in? (Accept several responses.) Finally, "O"— what are some options here? (Accept several responses.) Your ideas are so great, I'm sure they would be ready to move on to "P" and resolve this conflict!"

Divide participants into teams of six persons, making sure that each team includes more than one generation. Give each team a packet of S.T.O.P. cards. Tell them that two people should act out the situation given on one of the cards, then the entire team can talk about the S, T, and 0 steps that could be taken in this situation. Tell them to do this for all six cards. Arrange a signal such as a horn or whistle that you will sound every 3 minutes to tell them it's time to change to the next card.

Prayer table tent (10 minutes)

Purpose: To learn a prayer that can help in the process of resolving conflicts.

Gather the group and share this story in your own words:

There were two little girls who were just beginning to practice the fine art of name calling. "You stupid idiot!" one would say. The other would shout back, "Dummy dippy doo to you" and on it would go.

The mother tried nobly to get the upper hand on this, appealing to every authority she knew to nip this in the bud. Nothing seemed to work. Should she wash out their mouths with soap? Spank? Pray?

She decided to try prayer. So she composed a prayer that she taught her little ones to say. She required that they both take the time they needed to cool down before joining hands to say the prayer. And, that's what they got in the habit of doing. Sometimes, when they're on the go, they abbreviate it and say, "I'm sorry. Can we make a fresh new start?" But, most of the time they pray like this:

Dear Jesus, Thank you for my family
to live with heart to heart.
To hug, to smile, to laugh with,
we've been together from the start.
And for the times when we forget
how special we each are,
help us to let go...
and make a fresh new start! Amen

The prayer was meant for the little ones. But, before long, the mother was praying it and the father was requesting that they all pause for this prayer when things get out of hand.

Pass out copies of the prayer to each participant. Show the sample Prayer Table Tent you made, and invite them to make one to put on their table at home.

Directions for making a Prayer Table Tent

1. Color the Fresh Start Prayer with markers.
2. Fold a sheet of construction paper in half along the 12" side.
3. Fold under 2" on each 9" end of a sheet of construction paper.
4. Tape or staple the flaps so that the table tent stands.
5. Glue the Fresh Start Prayer to the front of the table tent.

CLOSING

Confession and forgiveness (15 minutes)

Purpose: To appreciate the gifts of confession and forgiveness.

Gather participants in a group for the closing. Distribute copies of your worship book and ask them to turn to the order for confession and forgiveness that you usually use in worship.

Say, "It's been great to see you practicing the S.T.O.P. process. I hope you'll use it every chance you get. God has promised to give us the strength to live in healthy relationships. He sent his Son, Jesus, to give us a perfect relationship with God and to model loving ways of living with each other. Because of Jesus, we can go to God to confess our weaknesses and our sins and to know that God is ready to forgive us and give us a fresh start."

Lead the group in praying the order for confession and forgiveness. If you like, close with a song or hymn on the theme of God's care for our lives, such as "What a Friend We Have in Jesus."

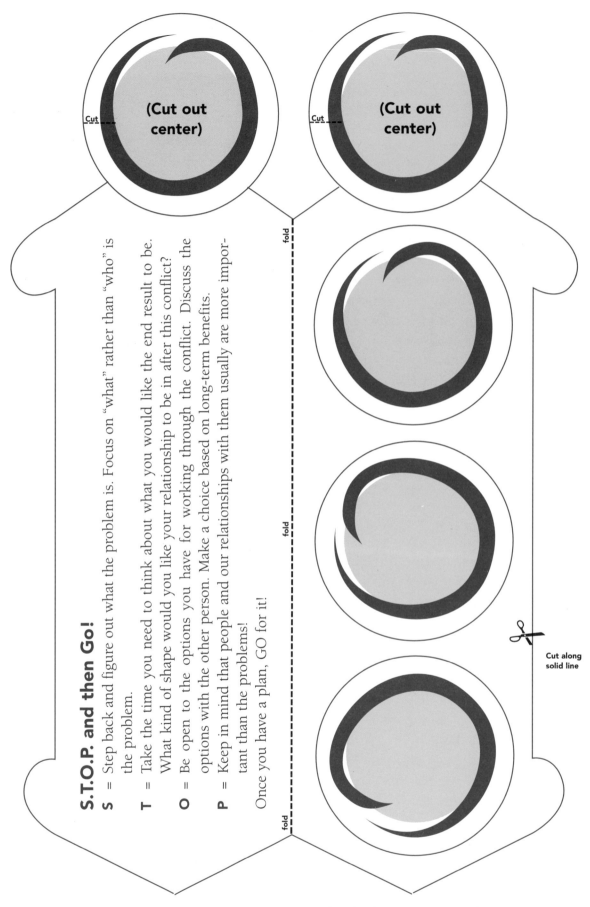

(Cut out center)

(Cut out center)

Cut

Cut

fold

fold

fold

S.T.O.P. and then Go!

S = Step back and figure out what the problem is. Focus on "what" rather than "who" is the problem.

T = Take the time you need to think about what you would like the end result to be. What kind of shape would you like your relationship to be in after this conflict?

O = Be open to the options you have for working through the conflict. Discuss the options with the other person. Make a choice based on long-term benefits.

P = Keep in mind that people and our relationships with them usually are more important than the problems!

Once you have a plan, GO for it!

Cut along
solid line

S.T.O.P. CARDS

Teacher: Where is your homework?

Student: I didn't do it.

Teacher: I can't believe you did this again! Don't you know you have to do this? Are you just lazy or what?

Student: I didn't feel like it.

Teacher: You're not going to master these fractions if you don't practice.

Student: Ah, who cares about fractions anyway?

Husand: I ran out of gas on the way to work today. Why didn't you put gas in the car when you were out last night?

Wife: I didn't know it was empty.

Husband: How irresponsible can you be? You can't just leave the car with an empty gas tank!

Wife: But buying the gas is your job!

Friend A: What are you doing wearing my red sweater? I only let you borrow that for one party!

Friend B: It looks so nice on me, I thought I'd wear it again.

Friend A: You can't do that. Give it back!

Friend B: Why are you so selfish? I'm never talking to you again.

Friend A: I didn't finish my science project. Let me put my name on yours and we'll tell the teacher it was a joint project.

Friend B: No way! I stayed up until 10:00 last night finishing this. I'm not putting your name on it.

Friend A: Come on. If I get a low grade in science, Mom will make me quit the soccer team. And it will be all your fault!

Friend B: Get away from my science project! You're no good at soccer anyway!

Mother: Who wrote down this phone message? I can't read the number.

Son: It was some guy who got your name from your office. He wants to place an order or something.

Mother: Well, I can't take an order if I can't call him, can I? You know I earn my money by the number of orders I place. This is costing me money! How can you be so irresponsible?

Son: It's not my fault. Tell your work people not to call here. Then this wouldn't happen.

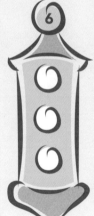

Youth: Where were you last Sunday? You promised to come to our concert and I looked for you.

Youth director: I guess I got too busy to make it.

Youth: But you promised! I even told my folks you would be there. It was pretty embarrassing when you didn't show.

Youth director: You should have known I might not be there.

Youth: See if I ever trust you again.

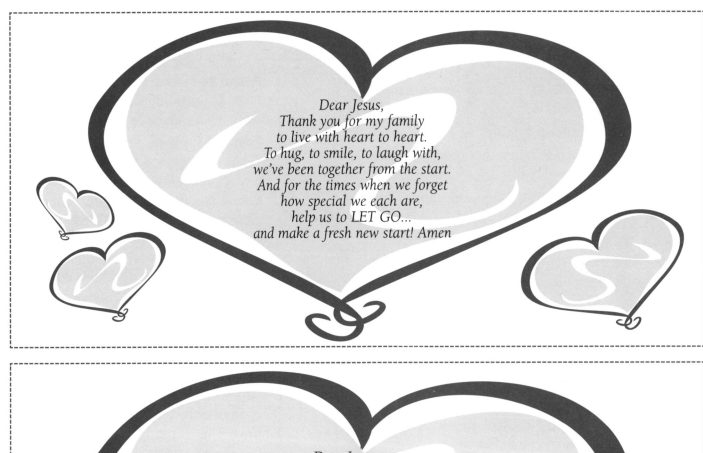

Dear Jesus,
Thank you for my family
to live with heart to heart.
To hug, to smile, to laugh with,
we've been together from the start.
And for the times when we forget
how special we each are,
help us to LET GO...
and make a fresh new start! Amen

Dear Jesus,
Thank you for my family
to live with heart to heart.
To hug, to smile, to laugh with,
we've been together from the start.
And for the times when we forget
how special we each are,
help us to LET GO...
and make a fresh new start! Amen

'N SYNC

PLAN FOR DAILY LIFE IN GOD'S PRESENCE

THIS INTERGENERATIONAL EVENT LINKS:

- The skill of exploring God's presence as we consider daily decisions;
- The faith practice of encouragement; and
- Asset 32, Planning and Decision Making.

KEY LEARNING POINTS

✔ As we plan the routines of our daily lives, God is there with us.

✔ The choices we make reflect our understanding of God's relationship with us.

✔ God cares for us in times of worry.

BACKGROUND FOR THE LEADER

The activity of daily life is perceived by many persons as stressful and hectic. For individuals of all ages, there are dozens of choices to make each day among a host of options that all appear to be good ways to enrich and uphold the quality of their lives. For those living with other family members, the chore of planning and coordinating schedules for a day or a week can be daunting.

The church has the privilege to help the children of God consider what they value in life and learn to make decisions based on those values. This event will help participants discover God's loving plan in the midst of their routines and encourage each other to consider faith-centered ways to plan the tasks of daily life.

KEY BIBLE TEXTS

You have looked deep into my heart, LORD,
and you know all about me.
You know when I am resting or when I am working,
and from heaven you discover my thoughts.
You notice everything I do and everywhere I go.
Before I even speak a word,
you know what I will say,
and with your powerful arm
you protect me from every side.
I can't understand all of this!
Such wonderful knowledge is far above me.

Psalm 139:1-6

But it is just as the Scriptures say,
"What God has planned for people who love him
is more than eyes have seen or ears have heard.
It has never even entered our minds!"
God's Spirit has shown you everything. His Spirit finds out everything, even what is deep in the mind of God. You are the only one who knows what is in your own mind, and God's Spirit is the only one who knows what is in God's mind. But God has given us his Spirit. That's why we don't think the same way that the people of this world think. That's also why we can recognize the blessings that God has given us.

1 Corinthians 2:9-12

Our God says, "Calm down, and learn that I am God!"

Psalm 46:10

EVENT SCHEDULE

Let's gather

    Beginning activities   **15 minutes**

Making faith connections

    Inside out   **15 minutes**

    Making choices   **10 minutes**

    Rhythms of ritual and routine   **10 minutes**

    The sands of time   **10 minutes**

    Break   **10 minutes**

    Prioritizing the process   **10 minutes**

    Water marks   **10 minutes**

    Pause and release   **10 minutes**

    Day by day   **10 minutes**

Closing

    Sealed with God's intent   **10 minutes**

MATERIALS NEEDED

Beginning activities

- One clear quart jar for each family unit or household
- Permanent markers or glass markers
- Plain paper, one sheet per family unit
- Crayons

Inside out

- Permanent markers
- Rocks that are about 2"-3" across, five rocks per family unit or household. Note: the rocks must be large enough to write on, yet small enough to fit inside the quart jar.
- Masking tape to mark the floor; or permanent markers and disposable plastic table cloths, one for each group of 15-20 participants

Making choices

- Pebbles that are about 1/2" across, four or five pebbles per person. You can purchase pebbles like this where aquarium supplies are sold.
- Small pieces of paper, one per person
- Pencils

Rhythms of ritual and routine

- Chart paper, 1/2 piece per family unit or household

- Markers, masking tape
- Aquarium gravel, 1 cup per family unit or household

The sands of time

- Fine sand, 2 cups per family unit. If necessary, you can purchase craft sand.
- Plain paper, one sheet per person
- Pencils, highlighter markers

Break

- Snack item of your choice

Prioritizing the process

- One quart jar that has two cups of fine sand in it
- One cup aquarium gravel
- Five 1/2" pebbles
- Five 2"-3" rocks

Water marks

- Large bowl or baptismal font with water
- Worship book
- Paper cups, one per family unit or household

Day by day

- Clear, self-adhesive vinyl, a 4"x6" piece for each person. Or, self-cling vinyl sheets can be used if these are available.
- Permanent markers

Sealed with God's intent

- Canning lids and sealing rings, one per family unit or household. These lids and rings must fit the quart jars.
- Bible verse circles (see preparation below)

PREPARATION

- Tend to the ministry of hospitality by providing name tags and making sure that there is comfortable seating for all participants.
- This event has a fast pace, and the individual activities are fairly brief. Be sure to have all materials ready to use and all preparations completed before the session begins.
- Create a round target for use on the floor that is at least 4' in diameter. You can create this with masking tape on the floor or permanent marker on a disposable plastic table cloth. Draw a heart in the circle in the center of the target. Draw four rings around this center, leaving about 10"

between rings. Make one target for every 15-20 participants.

- Invite a young person to make a computer poster of Psalm 46:10.
- Make Bible verse circles for the family jars. First, use a computer or typewriter to write 1 Corinthians 2:9, "What God has planned for people who love him is more than eyes have seen or ears have heard. It has never even entered our minds!" This verse must be small enough to fit inside a circle that is the size of the jar lid. Photocopy the sheet so there is one Bible verse circle for each family unit.

> **Throughout this session, small groups are called teams to differentiate them from the large group. Whenever you see the term *group*, it refers to all the teams together.**

LET'S GATHER

Beginning activities (15 minutes)

Purpose: To learn each other's names and be introduced to the theme of the event.

Greet participants as they arrive and ask them to make and wear name tags. Direct family units to the two activities you have prepared. Invite individual children, youth, and adults who come without other family members to work alongside other individuals as the "F.O.G. Family" (Family of God) throughout this event. However, consider each individual attending alone as a family unit, encouraging each one to complete the family jar activities.

Family signs and designs

Give one quart jar to each family unit or household and direct them to use permanent or glass markers to label it with their family name and then draw pictures that describe their family and the individuals in it (for example, a soccer ball, a piano, a mini-van, a pet, a tent, a heart, a smile, their house number).

Family name game

Have each family unit write the letters of their family name(s) in a vertical line alongside the left edge of a sheet of paper. Then, challenge them to write a word for each letter that describes an activity in which they are involved. (For example, the Thomas family might write: Tennis, Helping at food bank, Organ concerts, Making breakfast together on Saturday, Always on the go, Singing while doing dishes.)

As participants complete these two activities, gather as a large group. Introduce the theme for the day in the following way, "Today we will be talking about things that fill and shape our daily lives as families and households." Ask each family unit to introduce themselves to the group by standing, speaking their name(s), and telling the group the words on their Name Game sheets. Afterward, post the Name Game sheets on a wall as a "gallery of amazing families."

Pray together, "We give you thanks, loving God, for all your children gathered here today. Send your Holy Spirit to assure us of your presence in all the activities of our lives. Help us encourage each other to seek your will in our plans for each day. Bless this time together. Amen."

MAKING FAITH CONNECTIONS

Inside out (15 minutes)

Purpose: To identify the core values that shape and guide one's family life.

In the large group, comment, "There are many things about each household that can be observed by others, like the location of our home, the car we drive, our occupations, or the sports we play—things like the pictures you drew on the family jars. There are many other things about our families that very few people know, such as personal dreams, challenges, rituals, or priorities. There is someone, however, who knows us inside and out. God knows every thought and feeling."

Read aloud Psalm 139: 1-6. Ask the group to respond with, "God knows us inside out" after each verse.

You have looked deep into my heart, LORD, and you know all about me. **(Response.)**

You know when I am resting or when I am working,
and from heaven you discover my thoughts.
   (Response.)
You notice everything I do and everywhere I go.
   (Response.)
Before I even speak a word,
   you know what I will say,
   and with your powerful arm
   you protect me from every side. **(Response.)**
I can't understand all of this!
Such wonderful knowledge is far above me.
   (Response.)

Ask each family unit or household to choose five of the large rocks. Tell them to think of the five most important values they have—the guiding forces that shape their lives. (For example, God's love, working together, making time to play together, sticking together as a family, sharing with others, being honest.) Have them use permanent markers to write one core value on each rock.

Direct family units to gather around the target you prepared. If your group is large, have one target for every 15-20 persons. Ask them to use the target to help them think about their priorities. Tell them to first place the rock with the most important value or guiding force—the one that represents the heart beat of their family—on the heart in the center. They should then order the four other values or guiding forces in their lives by placing one rock in each ring of the target in the order of their importance.

When all have completed this prioritizing, invite them to step back and take a look at the "big picture." Without judging the placement of any rock, ask them to think about any changes they'd like to make in their own priorities. Encourage participants to discuss this within their families (or within the F.O.G. Family) as they put the five rocks in their decorated family jars.

Making choices (10 minutes)
   Purpose: To identify activities that take priority when making choices.

Give participants pencil and paper and ask them to number it from 1-5. Have each person think of the five activities in her or his life that are most important—the ones that take priority when choices have to be made. (For example, work, school, worship, family outings, exercise, time with friends, a favorite TV show.) Give each person five pebbles, one for each activity they have listed. Ask them to name aloud each activity on their list as they add the pebble to the decorated family jar.

Rhythms of ritual and routine (10 minutes)
   Purpose: To consider the role of repeated activities in daily life.

Comment that our lives are shaped by the major activities we choose to do, and that they are also shaped by the little things that happen each day—the routines—and those things that we repeat on a regular basis—the rituals. Ask the group to name some examples of daily routines that are important in their lives. (For example, bedtime prayers, grace at meals, hugs and kisses when saying hello or goodbye, eating a snack after school, checking the calendar of activities during breakfast, etc.) Then ask for some examples of rituals, important things that take place on a regular basis, but usually not every day. (For example, taking a walk on Christmas Eve to look at the lights in the neighborhood, going to sunrise service on Easter, using a special plate for the birthday person, visiting the cemetery on Memorial Day, stopping at the same ice cream shop on vacation each year.)

Next, give each family unit a half-sheet of chart paper and some markers. Invite the F.O.G. family to work on one chart as a team. Have them create two columns, one for "routines" or notable activities that are repeated in their homes everyday and one for "rituals" or special celebrations and events that have become mile markers or traditions in their homes. Challenge them to list as many as they can in each column.

Allow a few minutes for discussion, "How do routines and rituals create a sense of rhythm in our lives? What happens when routines are interrupted or rituals are changed?"

Give each family unit or household one cup of aquarium gravel to represent the role this rhythm plays in providing the ongoing beat of their family life. Invite them to pour it into their decorated family jar. Comment on how colorful the jars are becoming as they are filled with the variety of activities and events in their lives.

> **ASSET 32, Planning and Decision Making. Young person knows how to plan ahead and make choices. Congregations and outdoor ministry sites can build this asset by building a desire in children and youth to consider their plans through a "lens of faith" and make good choices based on their faith values.**

The sands of time (10 minutes)

Purpose: To reflect on the shared activities in daily life.

Ask participants to think of a typical Monday in their lives. Give participants a sheet of paper to make a detailed list of what happens in their lives on a Monday, beginning with the alarm and ending with crawling into bed. Encourage them to be as detailed as they can. Children who are in the pre-reading stage can draw pictures that highlight their activities. Then, provide highlighters that participants can use to indicate the activities that are common to other people in their household. Then, remind them of the five big-rock values they placed in their family jars. Have them put a check mark by activities on the list that reflect these values or guiding forces.

Conclude this activity by giving each family unit or household two cups of fine sand to add to their decorated family jars to represent the tiny details of daily life.

Break (10 minutes)

Serve a snack of your choice. Encourage participants to mingle and get better acquainted with each other.

Prioritizing the process (10 minutes)

Purpose: To consider how one's values, choices, and routines in life work together as choices are made.

Gather participants as a group. Do this demonstration, following the talking points given for each step.

1. Hold up the jar with two cups of sand in it. As participants have filled their family jars, they started with core values and guiding forces. Imagine what happens when we let the details of our daily routines set the stage for our planning and decision making.

2. Add the cup of aquarium gravel to the jar. When the daily details govern our lives, there is still room for special routines and rituals.

3. Add the pebbles to the jar, and then the larger rocks. As we can see, it can be a challenge to fit in the individual priorities and almost impossible to fit in the core values and guiding forces that are meant to give our lives focus and shape. In fact, lots of people get tired of trying to fit these into their lives and just quit trying. If we were truthful, each one of us has days when our jars are like this.

Invite them to reflect on how they are "filling the jars" of their own lives each day. Have teams of four or five persons discuss: "What does it feel like when we put the big rocks in place first? What does it feel like when we begin our planning with the sand?"

Read aloud 1 Corinthians 2:9-12. Say, "As people of faith, we rejoice that God has some big rocks for us—guiding plans and values for us to use each day. We know that each minute of the day is a blessing and a gift. How we plan to use these minutes can reflect God's love and forgiveness. The key is to put the big rocks in first—to cling to the values that are most important."

Water marks (10 minutes)

Purpose: To affirm one's baptismal faith as a guiding force in daily life.

Ask participants to gather in a circle around the bowl of water or baptismal font. Talk about the role of water in daily life and God's activity in the water of Baptism (claims us as God's child, brings forgiveness, salvation, faith).

Read aloud the section of the baptism service in your worship book that celebrates the newly baptized person's membership in God's family. Invite people to take turns remembering their baptisms by dipping their fingers into the bowl and making the sign of the cross on each other's forehead as they repeat these words, "Child of God, you have been sealed with the Holy Spirit and marked with the cross of Christ forever."

Ask the group to comment on the significance of living each day as a child of God. What difference does it make to see life through the lens of faith? What do we see?

Comment on our baptismal faith as a force that flows into every aspect of our lives. Invite a representative from each family unit or household to bring their jar to the baptismal font or bowl of water. Have each representative use a paper cup to fill their jars with water from the font to visualize the ability of faith to flow into every priority, activity, ritual, routine, and daily activity of their lives. Remark how grace frees us to go and do and be. Put the family jars on a table to be finished during the closing.

Pause and release (10 minutes)

Purpose: To learn to pause and release the worries of the day.

Have participants sit in pairs, back-to-back, on the floor. Suggest that sometimes the sand and the pebbles of our daily lives threaten to overwhelm us and we need to take a break and refocus—to pause and reflect. Point them to the words of Psalm 46:10 on the poster and ask participants to repeat the verse with you ("Calm down and learn that I am God."), saying it more softly each time until it is a whisper.

Ask partners to literally support each other as they rest on each other, pausing to reflect on God as master designer, life-giver, creator, and friend. Then ask them to think of ways they see God's presence and activity in their lives and how God's love for them influences the fundamental values they hold—the big rocks. After a few minutes have them turn toward each other and share some of their insights and ideas.

Day by Day (10 minutes)

Purpose: To make a reminder to look for God's presence in daily life.

Give one 4"x6" piece of self-adhesive vinyl or self-cling vinyl to each person. Write "Where did you see God today?" on the vinyl, using permanent markers. Illustrate the border of the vinyl with symbols of their faith (such as cross, heart, dove, rainbow).

Then, have the group look at the sheets where they described a typical Monday and ask, "So, where did you see God in that Monday you described?" (Possible sightings might include: in nature, in the loving-kindness of another, in good deeds, in expressions of faith, in the church or world.) Affirm all answers.

Tell participants to take the vinyl home, remove the backing, and stick it to a mirror, window, refrigerator door, filing cabinet, or somewhere else where they will encounter it on a daily basis. Encourage them to use this question to stimulate their own personal reflection and faith talk with other members in their household.

CLOSING

Sealing it with God's Grace (10 minutes)

Purpose: To remind participants of God's plan for their daily plans.

Say, "It's time to seal our jars in the same way that God seals our daily lives. Symbols of the "stuff" of our lives are contained in our jars—our values, individual choices, routines, rituals, and the activities of ordinary days. All of our lives are bathed in the waters of Baptism and as we seal the jar we remember what God tells us in 1 Corinthians 2:9, "What God has planned for people who love him is more than eyes have seen or ears have heard. It has never even entered our minds!"

Demonstrate how to place the metal lid and Bible verse circle on the jar and seal with the screw-on ring. Ask each family unit to seal their jar, take it home, and put it in a place where they will see it and be reminded of the values, individual choices, routines, rituals, and ordinary activities that make up the life of the faithful people of God who are washed in the waters of Baptism.

Invite all participants to join in a circle. Sing a song about God's presence, such as "Day by Day" and pray The Lord's Prayer as you close your time together.

EXPLORE THE WONDERS OF CREATION

THIS INTERGENERATIONAL EVENT LINKS:

- The skills necessary to work together on a common task;
- The faith practice of worship; and
- Asset 8, Youth as Resources and Asset 30, Personal Responsibility.

KEY LEARNING POINTS

✔ By asking good questions and discovering the answers together, we can work together to accomplish a common goal.
✔ God's awesome creation inspires us to praise the Creator.
✔ We are called to take personal responsibility for caring for God's creation.

📖 KEY BIBLE TEXTS

God looked at what he had done. All of it was very good!

Genesis 1:31

Our LORD, by your wisdom you made so many things; the whole earth is covered with your living creatures.

Psalm 104:24

BACKGROUND FOR THE LEADER

In the movie *The Wizard of Oz*, Dorothy may have made the Land of Oz famous, but it was God who created the land of aah's and ah-ha's. God, the Creator, created this world filled with wonders. God created little tiny fish that swim in the sea, giant-size moose that tromp through northern forests, butterflies that gather on garden flowers, wiggly worms, sparrows and, yes, God created mud. God filled the world with colors, textures, smells, and sounds. Each time we head outside we have an opportunity to see God's handiwork—no matter where we live. Learning to use our senses is rewarded with new findings and an opportunity to share with others. With a little help, we can easily become absorbed in seeing the aah's and the ah-ha's of God's creation.

The outdoor environment provides an opportunity for discovery and sharing. Every member of God's family has an opportunity to be an explorer, a leader, a scientist, and a storyteller. Each person is a resource as we learn and work together. The setting is ideal for giving young people useful roles in community activities and work. And to help each person experience first-hand how each of us is responsible for caring for God's creation. The experiences of being useful and being responsible are vital building blocks in the healthy development of our young people.

📄 EVENT SCHEDULE

Let's gather	
Gathering	**10 minutes**
Bop-Bippity-Bop	**20 minutes**
Making faith connections	
Who lives here?	**35 minutes**
Break	**10 minutes**
Critter Creation	**20 minutes**
Songs	**10 minutes**
Closing	**15 minutes**

MATERIALS NEEDED

Let's gather

- "Explorer" outfit for the group leader. A shirt from your area outdoor ministry site would be great—along with boots, a fun hat, binoculars, and a butterfly net. Encourage helpers to also dress as explorers.
- Name tags, markers

Who lives here?

- Who Lives Here? reproducible sheet on page 75.
- Pencils or markers
- Litter bags, gloves (optional)

Break

- Snack of your choice

Critter Creation

- Gather assorted art supplies for participants to use—yarn, string, felt, solid-colored fabric scraps, construction paper, glue, scissors, pipe cleaners, tape, toothpicks.
- One white paper plate per person

Closing

- Bibles for devotion leaders

PREPARATION

- Select the site for your adventure. Utilizing the Lutheran outdoor ministry site will help participants learn about the physical facilities of the camp/retreat/conference center and encourage further participation in the outdoor ministry programs offered in your area. If you do not have an outdoor ministry site nearby, select an outdoor site that offers opportunities for large and small group exploration. A wilderness area is not required.
- Make sure your site has an open area to use as your gathering place.
- Make sure your site has a trail of some kind for the Who Lives Here? activity.
- Make sure your site has tables or picnic tables. If you are in an area where the wind always blows, consider a closed shelter for the Critter Creation activity.
- Make sure you provide accurate, easy-to-read maps to your sites. Post signs to follow and to welcome.

- Restrooms should be located nearby. If you are using portable toilets, bring waterless hand sanitizer.
- Have plenty of drinking water and cups on hand to avoid dehydration and heat-related problems.
- On the day of the event have leaders and helpers at the site at least 45 minutes early to unload supplies. They also will need a few minutes to get oriented to the site and time for a group prayer.
- Fifteen minutes before the start of the event, guides and helpers should move to the parking area ready to help families get parked and unloaded. Keep an eye out for those little ones that can quickly pile out of the car and take off running before the adults have a chance to even unbuckle their seat belts.
- Set up a registration area. Have name tags for everyone. Name tags send a message that each person is important. There isn't any really good way to do name tags with children, but safety pins work well.
- Pack a first-aid kit and designate someone with First Aid and CPR certification to serve as the Health Care Specialist for the day. Be sure to have the number for the local emergency medical services (EMS) and access to a telephone.
- Make a copy of the Who Lives Here? reproducible sheet on page 75 for each person.
- Make a Critter Assignment Sheet for each team of four to six participants. Include several of the elements in parentheses on each one, but make no two the same.
  - This critter is a _____ (plant, mammal, fish, reptile, bird)
  - It lives _____ (on rocks on top of a mountain, on a dairy farm, underwater, in the desert, on a school playground, downtown New York City, etc.)
  - It _____ (gets stepped on a lot, is able to survive cold winters, has a beautiful flower that people like to pick, is something raccoons like to eat, etc.)
- Make a copy of the Awesome Praise reproducible sheet on page 76 for each person.

- Select leaders to help with the closing in advance so they have a chance to read their material and are comfortable with their role. An intergenerational leadership team is important as we show all of God's children (young and old) are valuable resources in the church.
- Arrange for a song leader or recorded music for the closing.

> **Throughout this session, small groups are called teams to differentiate them from the large group. Whenever you see the term *group*, it refers to all the teams together.**

LET'S GATHER

After all have made and put on their name tags, bring the group together for a heart-felt welcome, introduce individuals who are helping with activities, and thank the health care specialist.

The reason for your gathering is to help families grow in faith, so be sure you have an opening prayer. Lead a repeat-after-me prayer, which allows everyone to participate right off the bat. Keep it simple. Give thanks for the gathering time and for each person in our home families and in God's family. Give thanks for the time you have together to see, smell, touch, and hear the awesome wonders of God's creation. Give thanks for God's love and help us share that love with each other today. End with a hearty AMEN!

Other announcements should include the location of restrooms and a reminder that if they need anything they should just ask!

Bop-Bippity-Bop (20 minutes)

Purpose: To get acquainted with each other and begin to consider God's creation.

Gather the group in a circle and explain the directions for this game. Explain that the object is to stay out of the middle of the circle. Players will end up in the middle when they do not perform the assigned task correctly.

Directions for Bop-Bippity-Bop

1. A person ("IT") is selected to be in the middle. IT walks around the inside of the circle and stops in front of a player.

2. IT addresses the player by saying either BOP or BOP-BIPPITY-BOP. If IT says BOP, the person being addressed says nothing. If IT says BOP-BIP-PITY-BOP the person responds BOP before IT finishes saying BOB-BIPPITY-BOP. But if the person cannot do this quickly enough, IT and the person change places.

3. If you have a large group have several people in the middle so the game moves faster and involves more people. If someone gets stuck in the middle for too long, allow them to pick someone to take their place.

4. After a few rounds with just BOP-BIPPITY-BOP or BOP add additional elements to the game. IT can say BOP-BIPPITY-BOP, BOP, or any of these other elements. Add just one new element at a time:
- RABBIT: IT approaches a person and says RABBIT. The person and the two people on either side of the person must respond. The person in the middle of the threesome wiggles her or his nose or scrunches it up. The persons on either side hold up their arms to make the rabbit's ears. IT starts counting as soon as he or she calls out RABBIT. If IT can count to 10 before the threesome can do the actions, the last person still trying to do the action switches places with IT. Or if someone does the wrong actions they become IT. Nearby players can help be the judge if there is a question on who should be IT.
- ROBIN: When IT says ROBIN the person addressed uses her or his arms to create wings.

The players on each side lock hands to form a nest around the bird.

- FISH requires the center person to make a fish face and pretend to be a fish. Partners on the right and left become the waves.

- When you are ready to wrap up the game add MUD. When you yell MUD the entire group is stuck. They all act as if they are trying to pull their feet out of the sticky, icky mud.

5. Bring the game to a close with a round of applause for all the players. We want to generate a feeling of cooperation so have folks turn to the neighbor on the right and the left, introduce themselves and say, "Thanks for playing with me."

ASSET 8: Youth as Resources. Young people are given useful roles in the community. In our congregations and outdoor ministry sites, we can build this asset by identifying the interests, talents, and abilities of children and youth, and nurturing them through a variety of opportunities for leadership and involvement.

ASSET 30: Responsibility. Young person accepts and takes personal responsibility. We nurture this asset when we stress that children and youth are accountable to God, to themselves, and to others.

MAKING FAITH CONNECTIONS

Who lives here? (35 minutes)

Purpose: To work together to discover awesome things in God's creation.

Say, "The opening game let us 'meet' a few of the critters that live around here. But we only touched on a few of the many, many things that God created. We're going to become explorers and check out God's creation."

Take a few minutes to discuss the homes of various animals and birds that live in the area, hiking rules (stay on trails, do not pick flowers, we are visitors in this land), and any dangers of the area such as poison ivy, natural bodies of water, and off-limit areas.

Help participants form teams of four to six persons each. Be sensitive to family groups that want to stay together. Give each person a copy of the Who Lives Here? reproducible sheet. Explain that this is not a race, but a time for them to use their exploring skills and see the diversity of God's creation. Remind participants that each person on their team can be a help with the hunt by asking good questions and being good listeners—to each other and to the sounds of nature around them. Tell them that you expect each person to take responsibility for caring for God's creation. Give a litter bag to each team to use for their own trash and for any litter they see as they go along.

Give teams approximately 25 minutes to go exploring. Remind them again that the only thing they are collecting along the way is litter. Everything else on the list is a "see and leave" discovery. Before the teams leave, establish a signal such as a bell or a honking horn to signal when it is time to return, and encourage those who have a watch to also keep an eye on the time.

When the teams return, gather as a large group to go through the list to see what teams were able to find. Remember not to keep score. This reporting time is a time to recognize achievement, so be sure to praise participants for their findings.

Say, "The scavenger hunt allowed us to explore a bit and see what we might find in this area. We certainly did not have time to find out the names of the plants or birds, or to discuss in length their needs. Maybe you'll want to use this sheet as you go to new places for hikes, walks, and exploring adventures."

Break (10 minutes)

Allow participants 10 minutes as a break. Serve a simple snack of your choice and water to drink. Watch the weather. If it's cold, provide shelter for the group to warm up a bit. If it is hot, provide plenty of water and get folks to take a sit-down break.

Critter Creation (20 minutes)

Purpose: To work as a team to create an imaginative solution to an assigned task.

Gather the large group together for instructions. Say, "God, the Creator, certainly had a vivid imagination. Just think of how much fun God had creating an elephant, a whale, a sunflower, an ant, and the Black Angus cow. With each creation, God carefully thought about color and design. God thought about where the animals would live, what they would find to eat, what they should not eat, and the dangers they would face. God planned homes for the birds, the fish, and even the best place for the plants to survive. God created plants for mountain tops, underwater vegetation, and plants that people could eat. One might say God was a cutting edge designer! Now it's time for us to try our hands at being creators. Each team is going to invent a new critter."

Divide the group into teams of four to six persons. Allow families to stay together if they like. Say, "Each team will get an assignment sheet. The assignment is to create a new critter to be a part of this world, based on what you read on the sheet. We've gathered paper, glue, scissors, yarn, and other items you might need for your creation. When you are finished, place your creation on a paper plate, give it a name, and write its name on the plate."

When teams are finished, gather together as a large group and admire each creation. Read aloud Psalm 104:27, "Our LORD, by your wisdom you made so many things; the whole earth is covered with your living creatures."

Songs (10 minutes)

Start a song session, choosing fun and active songs related to God's creation. Introduce each song briefly to make the connections between the songs and God's awesome wonders.

CLOSING (15 MINUTES)

Say, "It has been a GREAT day! We had fun exploring and learning about God's many awesome wonders. We got to play a game, go on a hike, create a new critter, and now the time has come for us to gather and give special thanks to God for this day and all that God has created."

Review the key learning points of the event:

✔ By asking good questions and discovering the answers together, we can work together to accomplish a common goal.

✔ God's awesome creation inspires us to praise the Creator.

✔ We are called to take personal responsibility for caring for God's creation.

Before the closing, make any announcements you have, such as:

■ When you get ready to leave, please be careful in the parking lot. Drive slowly and watch for little ones.

■ Another big thanks to all of you for joining us today! Turn to your neighbor, give them a big smile and tell them "Thanks for coming today."

Cluster together around a campfire circle or on the ground. If possible, bring in props to help create a worshipful environment, such as a large cross, a table for an altar, a bright altar cloth, or candles.

Note to leader: To learn about servant events, high adventure camps, and volunteer service opportunities for youth and young adults, check out the *Journeys* catalog. It is available on-line at www.elca.org/dcm/camps/journey.html or by calling 800-638-3522, ext. 2593.

Who Lives Here?

Directions: This is a "see & leave" scavenger hunt, based on Genesis 1. Your goal is to see the items listed below and to take time as a family or team to discuss your findings. This is not a race. Stay together and work as a team.

- Find a place where you have both light and dark.

- Name three things that you could see in this area at night.

- Check out the sky—what shapes can you create in the clouds?

- Find three plants that have seeds.

- Find one plant that is yellow.

- Find a place where there is little sunshine. And find a place where the sun shines almost all day.

- Count how many different kinds of birds you see.

- Can you find any sea creatures? Or anything that swims?

- Choose an animal that you would be apt to find in this area. If you were this animal where would you live? What would you eat? Where would you go in case of danger?

- Look for three things that creep on the ground. Where are they going as they creep along?

- Humans are to care for the earth. Pick up 12 pieces of litter as evidence that we have not done a good job of caring for God's earth.

- What could we do to make this place a better home for animals?

- God said we need to take one day to rest. Can you locate a good resting place?

- Looking at tree branches, clouds, rocks, flowers, and the soil. Can you find the shape of a cross, a heart, and a smiley face?

Awesome Praise Devotions

Leader. The story of God's Awesome Wonders is told in Genesis. We used the story as the base for our scavenger hunt earlier today. Listen to the story of God's creation.

Reader 1. (Read Genesis 1:1-27, inviting participants to join in the phrase "and God saw that it was good" when you cue them.)

Leader. We've spent some time today learning about God's creation and the many animals God created in this space. We even got to create—making up new plants, animals, birds, and other critters. We made some really neat stuff, but we certainly are not able to create in the same way God did. God alone is the true Creator. Only God has the power to create life.

And when God created humans, God blessed them and gave them an important role to play. It's our responsibility to take care of the earth: to care for the plants, to protect the animals, to use our resources wisely, to keep the earth clean and healthy. Truly our God is an awesome God who created awesome wonders.

Song Leader. (Choose a song about God's greatness, such as "Awesome God" by Rich Mullins.)

Leader. God made each of us special and unique. We have different colored butterflies, in a variety of sizes, who live in many different places around the world, and we have people who come in different colors, in a variety of sizes, who live in many different places around the world. Listen to what David wrote about creation.

Reader 2. (Read Psalm 8.)

Leader. We have many different gifts and God wants us to use our gifts. Each human, each one of us, is special and unique. God created us this way! Remember to use your gifts as you explore God's creation and learn more about the Awesome Wonders that God has created.

Reader 3. Let us Pray. Creator God, you have given us so many, many blessings. We thank you for your Son, Jesus, who died to give us new life. We thank you for the neat things we were able to see today. Thank you for this time with family and with members of our church family. We ask that you help us to see ways we can use our gift to care for the earth and to help others learn about your Son Jesus and your love for us. O God, you have created many awesome wonders! We say thank you to you and pray in the name of your holy Son, Jesus the Christ. Amen.

Leader. The peace of the Lord be with you.

Group. And also with you.

Leader. Let us share that peace with a handshake or hug with those gathered here today. (Share the peace.)

Leader. Go in peace and serve the Lord.

Group. Thanks be to God!

INDIVIDUALLY WRAPPED AND WIRED

AFFIRM UNIQUE TALENTS AND ABILITIES

THIS INTERGENERATIONAL EVENT LINKS:

- The skills of naming and valuing one's own talents and the abilities of others;
- The faith practice of giving; and
- Asset 16, High Expectations, and Asset 40, Positive View of Personal Future.

KEY LEARNING POINTS

- ✔ God created each person in our families with unique gifts and abilities.
- ✔ We encourage each other to grow in faith by naming and calling upon the talents God has given us and holding high expectations for each other in using these gifts in the world.
- ✔ We "offer with joy and thanksgiving" what God has given to us—gifts and talents, time and treasures.

BACKGROUND FOR THE LEADER

We live in a culture that emphasizes shortcomings instead of abilities. Commercials on television and radio remind us that we are incomplete unless we consume or possess certain products. News reports too often point out the worst in human behavior. We measure, survey, and evaluate to find deficiencies. Yet, God has gifted us with wonderful talents. How can we help the people in God's family claim their gifts and do great things in the world with them, holding out a positive view of the future?

In the family of God, gathered in an outdoor

📖 KEY BIBLE TEXTS

*You are the one who put me together
inside my mother's body,
and I praise you
because of the wonderful way you created me.
Everything you do is marvelous!
Of this I have no doubt.
Nothing about me is hidden from you!
I was secretly woven together
deep in the earth below,
but with your own eyes
you saw my body being formed.
Even before I was born, you had written in your book
everything I would do.*

Psalm 139:13-16

But if you don't want to worship the LORD, then choose right now! Will you worship the same idols your ancestors did? Or since you're living on land that once belonged to the Amorites, maybe you'll worship their gods. I won't. My family and I are going to worship and obey the LORD!

Joshua 24:15

ministry site or a congregation, we can help each person name and develop these talents for service and growth. We can value each person's unique gifts and encourage everyone to give freely of them to a world in need.

Let's gather

Have you ever	**15**	**minutes**
Making faith connections		
Building a tower	**20**	**minutes**
Gift naming	**20**	**minutes**
Break	**10**	**minutes**
When good plans go wrong	**15**	**minutes**
Family mission statement	**15**	**minutes**
Overlap	**10**	**minutes**
Closing	**15**	**minutes**

MATERIALS NEEDED

Have you ever
- 8-10 individually wrapped soft candies or other small treat per person

Building a tower
- Assorted building supplies such as egg cartons, newspaper, brown paper bags, wire, masking tape. You need enough so that each person can choose one item.

Gift naming
- Small gift tags, like those put on Christmas packages, 1 per person
- Spiritual Gifts reproducible sheet on page 82
- Pencils

Break
- Snacks and beverage

When good plans go wrong
- Chart paper, markers, masking tape

Family mission statement
- Chart paper, markers
- Plain paper and markers for each family unit

Overlap
- Local newspapers, several pages for each pair of participants
- Highlighter markers, one for each pair

Closing
- Wrapping paper, one 12-inch square for each person
- Markers

PREPARATION

- Tend to the ministry of hospitality by providing name tags and making sure that there is comfortable seating for all participants.
- Make a copy of the Spiritual Gifts reproducible sheet for each person. You also may want to check out the spiritual gifts inventory on-line at http://www.mlc.edu. Download it and duplicate it for the participants if you'd like to use it as well.
- On a piece of chart paper, write these phrases: We (list individual names) have been given many gifts to enjoy and share, like (list gifts that individuals in your family have).

We believe that God has brought us together to (name some things your family enjoys doing together and how you reach out to help others.)

> Throughout this session, small groups are called teams to differentiate them from the large group. Whenever you see the term *group*, it refers to all the teams together.

LET'S GATHER

Have you ever (15 minutes)

Purpose: To help participants get to know each other better and to begin to sense the uniqueness of each individual in the group.

Form teams of four to six people and ask them to gather in a circle. Be sure that each team has more than one generation, yet be sensitive to family units who want to stay together.

Give each person eight to 10 of the individually wrapped treats. Say: "Each person in our group is special and unique. To help us find out just how unique we are, your team members will have a chance to tell about something they've done that they believe no one else has done. (For example, 'Have you ever played in a marching band? I have!') If someone else on the team has done the activity the person names, the person naming the activity will give everyone else on the team one of their treats. If no one else on your team has done the named activity, everyone will give the person speaking a treat. Each person on your team will get a turn to name an activity."

If someone runs out of treats, allow the team to decide how to handle the situation. After everyone has had a turn to name something and exchange treats, tell teams to pile all the treats in the middle of their team circles and share them.

While people are eating, invite each team to share the most unique thing mentioned in their team with the whole group. Say: "We are all truly unique. Beyond what we've done, we have different interests and abilities. Today we want to celebrate those things that make us special and how they make life richer in our families and in God's family."

Close this gathering time with a prayer, thanking God for the unique gifts, talents, and experiences of those gathered.

MAKING FAITH CONNECTIONS

Building a tower (20 minutes)

Purpose: To help participants experience the process of creating something by using the contribution of each person in the group.

Ask participants to go to the supply table where you have the assorted building supplies and to choose one item. Form new teams by having the group line up in order of birthdays—January birthdays at one end of the line, December at the other, and the rest, in order, in between. Beginning with January, have people form teams of five or six persons. Again, be sensitive to families who want to stay together.

Have teams move to a space where they can work together. Say: "Each team will now use the supplies that your team members have to build a tower. Your tower should be as tall as possible, while being as stable as possible. After five minutes, we'll have a contest and I'll try to blow each tower down. We'll then measure to see the tallest standing tower. You may only use the materials brought to the team—you can't trade with another team or go

to the supply table for additional supplies. And you must use everything your team members have brought. You cannot have anything left over."

After four minutes, remind teams that they have only a minute remaining. At five minutes, stop the building. Go around and try to blow down each tower. Measure those still standing to determine the tallest tower. Have the group applaud the efforts of all the teams.

Process the activity by discussing these questions in the large group:

- How did you feel as you considered the task and looked at what supplies your team members brought to the task?
- What steps did you take as you started building the tower?
- Did you have any challenges in using all the supplies you had?

Read aloud Psalm 139:13-16. Pause after each statement of what God has done and ask participants to respond with the phrase "Good job, God!"

Ask: "How do the words of this Psalm remind you of the activity we just did? What does it tell us about the people in our families, our congregations, and our communities? How does God look at the 'supplies' we bring to everyday life?"

Summarize by saying: "We need each other to experience the fullness of God's grace in our everyday lives. No matter what situation we face, God has given us what we need to get through it—if we are open to receiving the gifts and talents that each person can offer to help us."

Gift naming (20 minutes)

Purpose: To identify all participants as gifted individuals.

Note to leader: You can download and duplicate a Spiritual Gifts Inventory from the Midland Leadership Center at http://www.mlc.edu. If you have more than 30 minutes, use this inventory and the accompanying gift explanations to name each person's gifts. Be sure to talk about how you can use those gifts in everyday living.

Begin this activity in the teams formed for the

tower building activity. Give each person a gift tag. Ask a volunteer to read aloud Ephesians 4:4-13 from the reproducible sheet. Say: "We have many gifts represented in our families and in our congregation. God uses these gifts as we work together to make our communities healthy places in which to live. God expects us to use our gifts so that all the people in God's family can look forward to a bright future."

First, to help participants think more about God-given gifts, ask each person to think of one special gift God has given to her or him, write that on a gift tag, and stick it on her or his shirt. (If people seemed stumped, suggest some possibilities such as: good listener, faithful in prayer, welcomes newcomers, invites others to participate, speaks well in public, teacher, leader, encourager, organizer, artist, musician, etc.) Allow a few minutes for people in each team to tell each other about the gift they feel God has given them.

Next, give a copy of the Spiritual Gifts reproducible sheet to each person. Read through the groupings of gifts and explain them as needed. Tell teams to work together to name some of the gifts that they see in other people in your entire group. List their names in the "person" column.

When it seems most groups have named people with the gifts, say: "We're going to take a few minutes right now to tell those people we've named about their gifts. Send out representatives from your team to name gifts for others in the room. I'll give you a signal when we need to return to our teams."

Again, allow a few minutes for teams to share around the room. Call the teams back together and say: "Now we'll look at the people in our own teams. Work together to name at least two gifts for each person in your team. Be as specific as possible. You may share something you've noticed today or something you remember from a previous occasion." Tell them they will have eight minutes to do this.

Monitor the team's progress and remind them of the ending time. Call all the teams into the large group. Ask one person on each team to publicly name one gift for each person on the team.

Lead a discussion in the large group, using these questions:

■ How does it feel to have another person name a gift that he or she sees in your life?

■ How does it feel to tell someone about a special ability that you think God has given them?

■ What do you think would happen in our families and congregations if we strengthened our focus on naming the good things that God helps us do?

Say: "We have such talented people in our group. We can encourage each other to grow in faith by naming and calling upon the talents God has given us and holding up high expectations for each other to do exactly that!"

Break (10 minutes)
Serve a snack of your choice at this time.

When good plans go wrong (15 minutes)
Purpose: To consider how to respond when using our gifts and abilities causes us to feel uncomfortable or even gets us in trouble.

Ask participants to join again in the teams that they were in before the break. Tell team members to take turns sharing a personal story about a time when they thought they were doing the right thing, but then felt uncomfortable doing it or even got in trouble. As a team, identify the positive and the negative in each situation. Specifically, how did each person use a God-given gift or ability in the situation, even if the outcome was not the one hoped for?

After teams have shared a few stories, invite them to rejoin the large group to discuss these questions:

- Did any team help a team member discover a personal gift that he or she hadn't considered before?
- What would happen if we were to look at all the situations in life—both positive and negative—and try to identify how God's gifts are at work in those situations?

To close this activity, ask each team to write a one-sentence prayer that they could use to ask for God's help when they are in situations that cause them discomfort or get them in trouble with others. Have teams write this prayer on chart paper and post it on a wall for all to see.

Family mission statement (15 minutes)

Purpose: To help participants focus on how they use and develop each person's gifts in their families.

Have family units sit together. Encourage those who are single to gather together as a team. Say: "In our families—whether we live in the same household, or in different ones, whether we share the same last name or many—God has given us gifts and talents, time, and the money we earn. For the next several minutes, each family is going to create a mission statement—a statement about the gifts that God has given to you and what you want to do with those gifts."

Point out the phrases on the chart paper (see Preparation) that family units can use as thought starters. After 10 minutes, ask each family unit to share their mission statement with the entire group.

After family units share their mission statements with the large group, lead a discussion with these questions:

- How can you use this family mission statement to shape your lifestyle and the choices you make each day?
- If we were to write a family mission statement for the group of God's family gathered here today, what would it say?

Encourage families to take their mission statement home and put it up where it will be seen by all family members.

Overlap (10 minutes)

Purpose: To help participant teams consider the needs of the community and the gifts they have been given to meet those needs.

Have each person find a partner. Distribute pages of your local newspaper and a highlighter pen to pairs. Tell them to identify two or three needs of others that they find in the stories on their pages. Then ask them about what gifts God has given people to help meet those needs. Ask each pair to choose one need to share with one other pair.

Gather as a large group and ask:

- What keeps us from using our gifts in meeting needs in our community?

Say: "God has given us gifts so we can experience God's grace through each other. If we find a need, we can ask God to send us the gifts necessary to address it. If we find unused gifts, we can ask God to expand our vision for service."

CLOSING

Celebration (10 minutes)

Purpose: To help each person give an offering of her or his gifts.

Give a piece of gift wrap to each participant. Say: "We each have been given many gifts to help build up our own family and God's family. Use the gift wrap to create an offering. Shape or fold your paper however you like, and write down the gifts or talents, time, or other resources that God has given you to share with all of God's family."

After a few minutes, ask each person to bring his or her gift to the center of the group and read aloud gifts he or she will share with others. After each person reports, have the group respond: "We receive your gift with joy and thanksgiving."

Close the activity with prayer: "Creator God, you fill our lives with blessings. Help us use all that you have given us, our talents and gifts, our time, and our treasures to be a blessing to others and to show them your love. Amen."

If you like, ask participants to attach their gift offerings to a bulletin board, titled "We Have Gifts to Share," so that others in your site or congregation can see it.

SPIRITUAL GIFTS

All of you are part of the same body. There is only one Spirit of God, just as you were given one hope when you were chosen to be God's people. We have only one Lord, one faith, and one baptism. There is one God who is the Father of all people. Not only is God above all others, but he works by using all of us, and he lives in all of us.

Christ has generously divided out his gifts to us...Christ chose some of us to be apostles, prophets, missionaries, pastors, and teachers, so that his people would learn to serve and his body would grow strong. This will continue until we are united by our faith and by our understanding of the Son of God. Then we will be mature, just as Christ is, and we will be completely like him.

From Ephesians 4: 4-13

Gifts Groups and Examples	Person
Relationships: Listening, Discernment, Encouragement, Hospitality, Inviting	
Service: Mercy, Helping, Giving, Teaching, Advocacy	
Skills: Crafts, Music, Artistic Abilities, Writing, Technology	
Spiritual Nourishment: Prayer, Pastoring, Witnessing, Exhortation, Faith	
Leadership: Administration, Team Building, Networking, Delegating, Decision Making	

STRENGTH FOR THE JOURNEY

DISCOVER GOD'S PRESENCE IN ALL CIRCUMSTANCES

THIS INTERGENERATIONAL EVENT LINKS:

- The skills necessary for resisting negative influences in positive ways;
- The faith practice of study; and
- Asset 35, Resistance Skills and Asset 37, Personal Power.

KEY LEARNING POINTS

✔ We can cope with life's many challenges with a sense of confidence.

✔ As we study the stories of God's people, we can strengthen our ability to see God's active presence in all of our life's circumstances.

✔ We celebrate the strengths that individuals and families possess for handling difficulties in positive ways.

BACKGROUND FOR THE LEADER

The emotional and powerful story of Joseph and his family is as real today as it was thousands of years ago. Joseph trusted God completely. The God who took care of Joseph during his incredible ups and downs at home and in an unfamiliar land is the same God who guides us, directs us, and cares for us today in our complex society.

Congregations and outdoor ministry sites have unique opportunities to bring all the generations together to experience the holy stories of God's people in fresh ways and to provide opportunities for individuals to share their own faith stories. In this event, people of all ages will study together and nurture each other's faith, proclaiming God's guidance and presence in their daily lives. As they leave, they will feel more able to resist negative situations and have a stronger sense of control over their lives. These all are important building blocks for the healthy development of young people, and adults are important co-learners with them in this growth process.

📖 KEY BIBLE TEXTS

Don't worry or blame yourselves for what you did. God is the one who sent me ahead of you to save lives.

Genesis 45:5

We know that God is always at work for the good of everyone who loves him.

Romans 8:28

I will bless you with a future filled with hope—a future of success, not of suffering. You will turn back to me and ask for help, and I will answer your prayers.

Jeremiah 29:11-12

📖 EVENT SCHEDULE

Let's gather	**15 minutes**
Making faith connections	
The holy story	**20 minutes**
Bandages and blessings	**20 minutes**
I want to be like Joe/Jo	**10 minutes**
Break	**10 minutes**
Community energizer	**10 minutes**
Journey hoop	**20 minutes**
Closing	
A circle of blessing	**10 minutes**

MATERIALS NEEDED

Let's gather
- Name tags
- Dot stickers in five different colors
- Wall maps, one of the world and one of the U.S.

The holy story
- Children's Bible
- Pair of sandals
- Adhesive bandages
- Bowl of water

Bandages and blessings
- Faith Talk Questions reproducible sheet
- Envelopes, one per team of six persons
- Permanent markers, two or three per team
- Assortment of adhesive bandages, about 20 per team
- Smiley-face stickers, two or three per person

Break
- Ingredients for trail mix snack: toasted oat cereal, raisins, coconut flakes, chocolate chips, etc., in separate bowls
- Serving spoons
- Small paper cups
- Ice water or other beverage

Journey hoop
- Sturdy scissors
- Paper punchers
- White poster board
- Variegated and solid colored yarn
- Thin wood or metal hoops, 9-12 inch diameter, one per family unit
- Glue
- Variety of beads, glitter, sequins, puffy paints, etc.

Closing
- Hymnals: *This Far by Faith, With One Voice,* or *Lutheran Book of Worship*

PREPARATION

- Invite young persons in the congregation to make computer posters of the key Bible verses for the session.
- Create an environment that touches all the senses and reflects the theme of journey from the moment participants enter the gathering space to when they depart. Think about hospitality. Welcome the stranger!
- Prepare a table with name tags, markers, and a chart of "The Five Generations," each with a different color of dot.

  The Five Generations Present in Congregations Today:

  1900 -1924 The Founders/G.I. Generation (76 and older)

  1925-1944 The Boosters/Builders (56-75 years old)

  1945-1964 The Boomers (36-55 years old)

  1965-1981 Generation X/Busters (19-35 years old)

  1982-2003 Millennials/Bridgers (18 and younger)

- Place color dots on the table for participants to put on their name tags.
- Hang the world and U.S. maps on a wall or easel at a height all can reach. Locate and mark on the world map, Canaan (area of Jerusalem today) and Egypt.
- Secure six copies of the same Children's Bible or Bible storybook. Locate the story of Joseph. Divide the story into six key parts and mark one of these parts in each Bible. If you are expecting fewer than 24 participants, use only four Bibles and divide the story into fourths.
- Make a copy of the Faith Talk Questions reproducible sheet on page 89 for each person.
- Copy each of these assets on its own sheet of paper. See pages 11-12 for definitions. Use six different colors of paper. Make enough copies so that each person will have one sheet.
  - ✗ Asset 28, Integrity
  - ✗ Asset 30, Responsibility
  - ✗ Asset 35, Resistance Skills
  - ✗ Asset 37, Personal Power
  - ✗ Asset 39, Sense of Purpose
  - ✗ Asset 40, Positive View of Personal Future
- Prepare a focal point table for the event. Cover it with a bright, multi-colored cloth. Place on it a Children's Bible opened to the story of Joseph,

a backpack, pair of sandals, adhesive bandages, a map, sample Journey Hoop project, and a bowl of water.

■ For Journey Hoops, cut circles of poster board that are 1" in diameter smaller than the hoops. Each family unit will need one.

LET'S GATHER (20 MINUTES)

Greet participants as they arrive. Direct them to the table to make a name tag. Ask them to place a colored dot on their name tag that matches the dot next to the generation into which they were born as shown on the chart you prepared.

> **Throughout this session, small groups are called teams to differentiate them from the large group. Whenever you see the term *group*, it refers to all the teams together.**

Direct participants to the two maps. Invite individuals to write their initials on the location on either map that represents the farthest he or she has traveled from home. People of all ages find maps fascinating. A map makes an old, old story more real! The map is also a means of connecting folks in your faith community through conversations about their journeys.

Direct everyone to a circle of chairs. Invite children, and anyone else, to sit on the floor inside the circle.

Acknowledge the number of generations gathered for this event. Rejoice if you have all 5 generations (all 5 colors of dots) represented! Ask who is willing to share the fact that they are the oldest and "wisest" person present. Cheer and clap! Acknowledge this person(s) as an elder in the community with years of experience and many faith stories to share. Identify the youngest one present and/or someone who is pregnant. Celebrate all the generations gathered and this opportunity to pass on the faith from one generation to another!

Say: "Today we are going to talk about life's journeys and adventures, recognizing that God is always with us and all things work for good for those who love God. We will study God's stories and share our stories."

Give the following instructions: "To get acquainted, each person will say, "My name is _____ and I am going on a journey. I am bringing a _____. The item you list must begin with the same letter as your first name." Leader begins. When all have had a turn, ask everyone to cover their name tag. Ask for a volunteer to go around the circle and name each person and the item he or she is bringing! Of course give lots of help! (Hint: To ask each person in the circle to repeat the name and item of the persons proceeding them often produces too much anxiety and spoils the fun!) If your group is very large, you may want to divide into teams of 12 to 15 persons for this activity.

Offer an opening prayer for your time together. Thank God for the many ages of people gathered for your journey of studying and sharing. Ask that the Holy Spirit guide your learning and your fellowship together.

> **Leaders often express reservation and anxiety about leading intergenerational events. Invite children to sit on the floor within a circle of caring adults. Provide materials for a simple, quiet activity. Children are able to listen and be busy at the same time! Young ones will feel safe and welcomed!**

MAKING FAITH CONNECTIONS

The holy story (20 minutes)

Purpose: To study the story of Joseph.

Guide participants to form six teams, or four teams if your group is less than 24 participants. Combine family units and single persons to form these small teams.

Say: "Today we are going to study the familiar

Joseph story found in the Old Testament. Everyone will have a part to play. Each team will receive a Bible with a small section of the Joseph story marked. Your team is responsible for creatively acting out your section of the story. You will have 5 minutes to come up with your part of the story!" Give each group the Children's Bible with their section marked.

When teams are prepared, gather as a group in your large circle and begin reading the Joseph story aloud from the Children's Bible. Read one section and then stop. Signal the appropriate group to act out that segment of the story. Continue until the entire story is read and acted out.

Bandages and blessings (20 minutes)

Purpose: To share insights into the Joseph story and personal faith stories.

Ask everyone to again gather into their small teams. Direct them to pull their chairs close enough together to clearly hear one another. Give each group an envelope that contains 15-20 various size adhesive bandages and enough smiley-face stickers for each participant to have two or three. Have permanent markers available for them. Give each participant a copy of the Faith Talk Questions reproducible sheet from page 89.

As leader, read aloud the questions on the sheet to the entire group. Ask everyone to not talk for a moment while they reflect on the questions. Explain that this personal thinking time helps each person be a better listener! Wait about 30 seconds. Then tell teams that they have about 15 minutes to discuss the four questions on the page.

Announce when there are 2-3 minutes of sharing time left. If a group finishes early, suggest they talk about a time when they were lost.

Say, "Let me see a show of hands of those who have a perfect family!" (Expect some giggles and hopefully no one's hands will go up!) There were no perfect families in the Bible either. We are not that different from Joseph and his family, are we? And like Joseph, God is with us, guides us through life's difficulties, and makes everything work for good."

"Strong families today have crisis, stress, conflict, and problems—just like Joseph's family. But strong families and individuals know that they are never alone. They know when to ask for help. They know how to forgive. They know God is always with them, every step of the way."

ASSET 35: Resistance Skills. Young person can resist negative peer pressure and dangerous situations. In our faith community, we can build this asset by equipping children and youth with the skills, confidence, and strength that only God can give to resist peer pressure and potentially dangerous situations.

ASSET 37: Personal Power. Young person feels he or she has control over "things that happen to me." In the family of God, we can encourage youth to grow in their understanding of Philippians 4:13, "Christ gives me the strength to face anything."

I want to be like Joe/Jo! (5 minutes)

Purpose: To identify some of the building blocks of healthy development that are part of Joseph's story and ours.

Say: "Joseph had many of the positive qualities that a person needs to be caring and responsible in society. Today we call these qualities 'developmental assets.' They are like building blocks for healthy lives, and the more we have the better."

Read the six assets you have prepared on sheets of colored paper. (Assets 28, 30, 35, 37, 39, 40.) Distribute the colored sheets, one asset to each participant.

Say: "Stand up and find a partner. The other person must have an asset sheet that is a different color than yours and a dot on her or his name tag that is a different color than your own!"

After all have found a partner, have them discuss

the following questions:

1. How did Joseph demonstrate this particular quality in his life?
2. How have you experienced this asset in your life?

Break (10 minutes)

Invite participants to take a break and make themselves a customized cup of trail mix from the ingredients you have set out in separate bowls.

Community energize (10 minutes)

Purpose: To become better acquainted and share personal stories with each other.

1. Divide participants into two teams. Have one team form a circle, facing out. The other team then forms a circle around them, each person facing a person in the inner circle.
2. Ask participants to introduce themselves to their partners. The leader reads one of the phrases listed below and asks pairs to share their answers.
3. Instruct participants in the outer circle to move two spaces to the left. Repeat introductions and read another phrase to discuss. Repeat as many times as desired, varying which circle moves, the number of spaces, and the phrase.
4. Phrases to use:
   - The farthest from home you have traveled.
   - Something you recycle.
   - A scar you have.
   - Something you feel strongly about.
   - A time you were lost.
   - Describe your favorite pair of shoes.
   - Something you could teach someone else.
   - Something you want to learn.
   - What you look forward to each day.
   - Your favorite Bible story.
   - Name someone who really cares about you.
   - One way you make a difference in the world.

Journey hoop (25 minutes)

Purpose: To make a creative reminder of our faith journey as a member of God's family and our family units.

Show everyone the sample of the finished craft as you walk through the instructions.

Directions for making a Journey Hoop:

1. Instruct each person to trace around one shoe on poster board. (Offer to assist anyone who may have difficulty in completing this task or the cutting activity)
2. Provide sturdy scissors to cut out each traced shoe.
3. Provide craft materials in a central location for participants to decorate their shoes. Have them write their names on their shoes.
4. Provide each family unit with a hoop and a length of variegated yarn to completely wrap the hoop. If a person is single, suggest they invite a friend or a grandchild to send them an outline of their shoe to add to the hoop later! Or continue this activity at home when friends and grandchildren come to visit!
5. Provide each family unit with a circle cut from poster board. Suggest they write in the circle one of the key Bible verses or "God is with us every step of the way."
6. Provide solid colored yarn to attach the center circle and the shoes to the hoop as illustrated. Paper punches will be needed to complete this activity.

Option: A simple alternative activity is to invite everyone to trace and decorate their footprint with sidewalk chalk in the parking lot, entrance way, courtyard, or camp basketball court. What a great way to create interest in "Faith Family Style: Generations Growing Together!"

After the Journey Hoops are completed, gather as a large group. Say, "Every day we learn more about how faith is nurtured through acts of service and intergenerational service projects. Think of

Yarn

Poster board circle

God is with us every step of the way

Hoop

Sam.

Karen

Paul:

members. It helps us resist negative influences and it gives us a sense of control over the things that happen to us. It also creates a power to reach out to the community. The idea of a circle of power is described in John Neihardt's book, *Black Elk Speaks*, 'Everything the power of the world does is done in a circle. The sky is round like a ball, and I heard that the earth is round like a ball; and so are all the stars...The life of a man is a circle from childhood to childhood, and so it is in everything where power moves...' "

Read aloud Psalm 78:1-4:
My friends, I beg you to listen as I teach.
I will give instruction
and explain the mystery of what happened long ago.
These are things we learned from our ancestors,
and we will tell them to the next generation.
We won't keep secret the glorious deeds
and the mighty miracles of the LORD.

ways to transfer your experience at this event into an act of service for others." Have participants call out things they might do, such as: fill shoe boxes with toiletry items for the homeless and needy; sponsor a drive to collect old shoes and polish, clean, and brighten them up with new shoe laces. Ask for the Holy Spirit to direct everyone's serving!

CLOSING

A circle of blessing (10 minutes)

Gather everyone once again into a circle of chairs placed around the altar or focus table. Ask everyone to sit in the chairs according to their generation or their "color dots," going from eldest to youngest.

If there is time, invite participants to share one thing they enjoyed or learned during this time together.

Say: "In their book, *Secrets of Strong Families*, John DeFrain and Nick Stennet talk about a circle of power in families. They say this circle of connections energizes and strengthens individual family

Using guitar or piano teach and lead the song, "I'm Going on a Journey," page 115, in the hymnal *This Far by Faith*. Or choose another hymn or song about God's guidance through life.

Ask everyone to stand. Invite each person to come forward and dip a finger into the bowl of water and make the sign of the cross on her or his forehead. Continue singing until everyone has had a turn.

Conclude with, "Thank you Lord, for creating families and the unique individuals that give them life and breath. We are humbled by your presence, power, and activity in our lives. We are reminded that no matter what life brings, in you, all things are for good through your Son, Jesus Christ. You promise to walk with us, hold us in your mighty hands. God be with us on our journeys, every step of the way. Go in peace and serve the Lord! "

The people respond, "Thanks be to God!"

Small, inexpensive Footstep Pins are available through religious catalogues or in many religious book stores. If your budget allows, purchase these as departing gifts for the participants.

FAITH TALK QUESTIONS

1. What feelings and emotions did Joseph and his family experience? Name as many as you can! Write some of these words on the adhesive bandages with permanent marker.

2. When have you felt some of these same emotions? Choose one or two of the bandages that have these feelings written on them. Put them on yourself.

3. How is your family like Joseph's?

4. What were Joseph's special gifts? What is a special gift or ability God has blessed you with? Place a smiley-face sticker on each bandage you are wearing.

20/20 VISION

EXAMINE VALUES AND CHOICES IN DAILY LIFE

THIS INTERGENERATIONAL EVENT LINKS:

■ Skills for discerning priorities and upholding them with integrity;

■ The faith practice of serving; and

■ Asset 28, Integrity.

KEY LEARNING POINTS

✔ Each individual person in the family is important and greatly valued.

✔ How we set priorities, plan, and make decisions says a lot about what we value and our integrity as a child of God.

✔ May our outreach to others reflect our journey as a child of God—chosen, called, equipped, and blessed.

📖 KEY BIBLE TEXTS

With all your heart you must trust the LORD and not your own judgment. Always let him lead you, and he will clear the road for you to follow.

Proverbs 3: 5-6

📋 EVENT SCHEDULE

Let's gather	20 minutes
Making faith connections	
Hand bouquet	20 minutes
Juggling it all	10 minutes
Hot and cold	15 minutes
SON glasses	15 minutes
Break	10 minutes
Closing	30 minutes

MATERIALS NEEDED

Let's gather

■ Solid color twin-size flat sheet or 45" x 60" piece of plain fabric

■ Fabric markers in bright colors

■ Materials for hanging the fabric banner for worship time

■ CD or tape of Christian music; CD or tape player

Hand bouquet

■ Bright-colored poster board, 9-inch square for each person

■ Floral wire, 12-inch piece for each person

■ Florist's green foam, 3-inch cube per family unit (or a piece of play clay about the size of a tennis ball)

■ Gift wrap ribbon in various colors, 18-inch piece per person

■ Tissue paper, 1 sheet per family unit

■ Bottom half of a quart or pint milk carton, 1 per family unit

■ Markers, scissors, tape

Juggling it all

■ Large balloons, inflated, 3 balloons for each team of 6 to 8 participants

Hot and cold

■ Bible

■ Book of matches

■ Chart paper, markers

SON glasses

■ SON glasses patterns

■ Posterboard

■ Yarn or string or craft sticks

- Scissors, paper punches
- Markers, pencils

Break
- Snack

Closing
- Volunteers to help with the closing
- Table and cloth to cover it
- Three candles; matches
- Standing cross for table top
- Bible
- Home Devotions reproducible sheet on page 97

PREPARATION

- Tend to the ministry of hospitality by providing name tags and making sure that there is comfortable seating for all participants.
- At several points in this event, it is suggested that you play some Christian music as the group does an activity. Make sure that your CD or tape player has enough volume to be heard easily in your space.
- Ask a group of people to pray for each family that will be attending the 20/20 Vision event. Pray that God's Word and amazing love will touch the heart of each person. Pray also for the leaders of this gathering, that they would be filled with energy, wisdom, and discernment.
- Be sensitive to those with physical needs that may require adaptations in the activities.
- Have a camera handy to capture some pictures.
- On the sheet or fabric, write in large letters: We're All God's Family.
- On a piece of chart paper, write the following instructions:
  - ✗ Palm—write your name
  - ✗ Thumb—write your favorite sport or activity
  - ✗ Pointer—write your favorite food
  - ✗ Middle—write one way you reach out to others
  - ✗ Ring—write the name of someone who has taught you about God
  - ✗ Pinkie—write the name of someone you admire for serving others
- Make a sample hand bouquet and a sample pair of SON glasses.

- For SON glasses, draw the shape of the front of a pair of glasses, making the frames at least 1" wide. Make patterns for participants to use. Don't worry about the side pieces that go over one's ears. Participants will tie yarn on the frames so the glasses can be tied behind their heads or staple frames to a craft stick to hold them in place. See drawing on page 97.
- Plan to recruit volunteers to help with the closing worship. As you read through the plan on page 95, note places where leaders are needed. Make a sign-up sheet for these needs and have it at the name tag table.
- Make one copy of the Home Devotions reproducible sheet on page 97 for each family unit.

> **Throughout this session, small groups are called teams to differentiate them from the large group. Whenever you see the term *group*, it refers to all the teams together.**

LET'S GATHER (20 MINUTES)

Stretch the bed sheet or fabric on a table near the entryway. As participants arrive, invite each person to sign his or her name on the sheet with a fabric marker. Encourage creativity. Invite participants to draw pictures and symbols of God's love between the names. This banner will be used later during the closing time.

As people are working, recruit a few volunteers to take part in the closing worship.

After all have added their names, hang the banner in the area where your closing for this event will be held. (After the event, hang it in a prominent place to remind people of their time together as God's family.)

After everyone has gathered, gather the group and welcome them in the name of the Father, and the Son, and the Holy Spirit. Tell everyone how great it is to gather as God's family. Introduce staff and leaders.

Tell participants to move around and form "huddles" by holding hands with the number of people that you call out. After each huddle is formed, allow time for participants to introduce themselves to the others in their huddle and for each person to answer the question from below that you give them. As participants form new huddles, encourage them to join huddles with different people. (Your youngest participants may want to be a buddy with an older sibling or parent for this activity.)

Huddle descriptions:

1. Huddles of 4 people: What is your favorite flavor of ice cream?
2. Huddles of 7 people: What is your favorite thing to do when you aren't working or at school?
3. Huddles of 3 people: Who is your favorite person in the Bible?
4. Huddles of 5 people: What is your favorite way to help, or serve, others?

Invite everyone to have a seat after the last huddle. Thank them for taking the time to reach out a hand to others in the group. Comment: "Our time together in Christian fellowship is important. As we have warmed up our hands and our voices, now let's warm our hearts by linking our hands and our hearts in prayer."

Lead this opening echo prayer:

Leader	Group
Dear Jesus	*Dear Jesus*
Thank you for this day	*Thank you for this day*
Thank you for bringing us here together as families	*Thank you for bringing us here together as families*
together as friends.	*together as friends.*
You are awesome.	*You are awesome.*
We love you.	*We love you.*
Thank you for loving us!	*Thank you for loving us!*
Amen.	*Amen.*

Music is such a great way to warm hearts and build community. Plan to sing one or two songs before the group moves into the next activity. Choose something easy to learn or very familiar—lean toward songs that children can easily participate in.

MAKING FAITH CONNECTIONS

Hand bouquets (20 minutes)

Purpose: To make a creative image of the individuals in each family unit.

Each family unit will make one Hand Bouquet.

Directions:

1. Give each person in the family unit a 9" square of poster board.
2. Trace one hand. Cut out the hand tracing and label it with markers, following the directions you wrote on the chart paper (see Preparation). Individuals may want to create hands for others in their family or to add these later at home.
3. Tape a piece of wire on the hand to give it a "stem." Tie some ribbon around the wrist area.
4. Put a piece of florist foam or clay in the bottom of a pint or quart milk carton that has been cut in half.
5. Stick all the wires in the foam or clay. Wrap the carton in tissue paper.

The Hand Bouquets will be placed on the altar for the closing worship.

Juggling it all (10 minutes)

Purpose: To consider the many priorities and demands in life.

Divide participants into teams of six to eight persons. Make sure each team has more than one generation represented. Be sensitive to family units who want to stay together.

Tell teams to imagine that they are a family. Give each team one balloon. Instruct them, when the music begins, to keep the balloon up in the air. Each person should have a hand in keeping the balloon up. After one minute, stop the music and ask teams to keep the balloons quiet.

Next, add a second balloon to each team. As you do, comment on all that we juggle in our lives every day—schedules, activities, work, school, friends, family, chores. Invite team members to list for each other a few of the things that they are juggling. Then, as the music begins, challenge them to keep two balloons in the air. After one minute, stop the music.

This time, have everyone put one arm behind their back and add a third balloon. Begin the music, then stop it after one minute. Comment on how we can get overloaded and out of balance, kind of like using just one arm. Sometimes we need to look again at our priorities, so that as a family, we strive to make sure we are doing the things that reflect what we think is most important in life.

Ask each team to discuss:

- What are the most important things that we do?
- What causes us to feel cluttered, too busy, stressed, tired, burned out?
- How could we change?

Ask teams to join together as a large group. Say: "Jesus came to bring us life and he wants us to live abundantly, but he does not want us to be on overload. Jesus would spend time with the large group (feeding the 5,000!). Then he would spend time with the team, a smaller group (his disciples). Then he would have a brunch with a few close friends (Mary and Martha). And then he would spend time alone (solitude and serenity). Jesus knew the importance of balance. He challenges us to look at what takes priority in our lives, as individuals and as a family. As we're planning our lives, we need to have balance and integrity, acting on what is important and standing up for what we believe."

End this time by inviting all teams to join together in a large circle and keep all of the balloons in the air. We're in this together—let's help and support each other! Let the music and the balloons begin!

> **ASSET 28: Integrity.** Young person acts on convictions and stands up for her or his beliefs. Congregations and outdoor ministry sites can build this asset by nurturing a sense of identity and belonging to God's family and inspiring an inner strength and commitment to act accordingly.

Hot And Cold (15 minutes)

Purpose: To examine the effect of the mixed messages we send and receive in our daily lives.

Without saying the name of the game, ask for a brave soul who will leave the room and go into a "sound-proof booth." As the person leaves, lift up their name and clap for them: "Let's hear it for _____!"

While the person is out of the room, review how to play the game, Hot and Cold. An object is hidden and then the person who has left comes back in and tries to find the item. When he or she is close to the item the other participants call out, "Hot;" when he or she is far away the others call out, "Cold."

Then explain that this game will be played a little differently. Divide into two groups by asking each person to turn to the person next to him or her and decide who will be on Team 1 and who will be on Team 2.

Say, "Team 1, raise your hands. You will be trying to send the person to a Bible. (Place a Bible in one place). Team 2, raise your hands. You will be trying to send the person to a book of matches. (Place a book of matches in a place far from the Bible.) What makes this so different is that Team 1 and Team 2 will be doing this at the same time. We will be watching the journey of the person trying to find an item, not knowing that the group is divided."

Ask the person in the hall to come back into the room. Explain the basic Hot and Cold game, without telling that there are two objects or two teams. Then begin the game. After about 30 seconds, stop the game and ask the person how he or she feels and if he or she thinks there is a good chance of succeeding.

Then explain to the person how the game was set up. Have Team 1 raise their hands. Tell the person that this team was sending him or her to the Bible. Have Team 2 raise their hands. Tell the person that this team was sending him or her to the book of matches. Thank the person for this great effort, and invite him or her to take a seat as the group applauds.

Ask these questions:

■ What did you learn from playing this game? (Accept all answers.)

■ What did this game tell you about mixed messages?

■ What mixed messages do we receive each day about serving or reaching out to others? (Media says to look out for self, indulge self. Gospel says to reach out and meet the needs of our neighbors.)

Next, say: "Team 1, your job was to send the person to the Bible, God's word for our lives. Team 2,

your job was to send the person to the book of matches, the vices in our lives and the things that cause us to make poor decisions. As followers of Jesus, we want to hear a clear message. Jesus said, 'Do you want to know the truth? I am the way, the truth, and the life! Without me, no one can go to the Father (John 14:6).' "

Also read aloud Proverbs 3:5-6 with the group.

Say: "We want to listen to God. We want to see clearly as if we were looking through the eyes of Jesus. This will affect our plans and decisions. It will have an impact on how we see ourselves and others. It will have a tremendous influence on how we serve and reach out to others. So be on guard for mixed messages. Don't let them fool you. You are a child of God!"

SON glasses (15 minutes)

Purpose: To add an imaginative dimension to the closing worship.

Tell participants that each of them needs a pair of SON glasses for the closing worship time. Show the sample of the glasses that you made while you give the directions.

Directions for making SON glasses:

1. Trace around the SON glasses pattern on poster board. Cut out the glasses.

2. Write "Looking at the world through the eyes of

Christ" across the top.

3. Decorate the rest of the frames with markers as desired.

4. Punch a hole in each side of the frame. Tie a 12" piece of yarn to each hole. Or, staple a craft stick to one side to hold up frame like "opera glasses."

5. To wear the glasses, tie the yarn in a bow behind the head.

Set these aside for the closing as participants finish and take their break.

Break

Before you begin the break, explain that the group will gather back together for the closing worship after the break. Recruit a few people to help set the room arrangement during the break. Tell participants that you will start the music when it is time to gather for the closing. Remind participants to bring their Hand Bouquets and SON glasses. Invite everyone to take a break. Encourage people to reach out and meet those that they do not know.

CLOSING (30 MINUTES)

During the break, set the area for the closing worship:

■ Use a large table for an altar area. Cover it with a cloth and put a candle and a cross on it.

■ Hang the sheet or fabric with all the names behind the table.

■ Put chairs in a horseshoe shape by the table.

At the end of the break, begin the music and invite participants to sit with their family units in the horseshoe.

Closing worship

Welcome: Tell the group that it is a joy to gather as families and that it has been fun to be a part of all the activities leading up to worship. What a blessing it is to gather now to praise and thank God.

Opening: Gather the group with the words "In the name of the Father, of the Son, and of the Holy Spirit" as you light the candles.

Song: Ask song leaders to lead *This Little Light of Mine.*

1. *This little light of mine, I'm gonna let it shine.*
This little light of mine, I'm gonna let it shine.
Let it shine, let it shine, let it shine.

2. *Hide it under a bushel, no, I'm gonna let it shine,*
Hide it under a bushel, no, I'm gonna let it shine,
Let it shine, let it shine, let it shine.

3. *Don't you try to "phew" it out, I'm gonna let it shine,*
Don't you try to "phew" it out, I'm gonna let it shine,
Let it shine, let it shine, let it shine.

Prayer: The person or group leading the prayer should pray from the heart that God will look upon all families and individuals gathered. Remember the other families not present. Ask God to take the lessons from this event and the Scripture spoken and plant them in everyone's heart.

Scripture: Read aloud the parable of *The Good Samaritan* in Luke 10:25-37. Have a group of people act this out as it is read.

Offering: Sing *He's Got the Whole World in His Hands.*

1. *He's got the whole world in His hands,*
He's got the whole world in His hands,
He's got the whole world in His hands,
He's got the whole world in His hands.

2. *He's got you and me Brother in His hands,*
He's got you and me Sister in His Hands,
He's got you and me Brother in His hands,
He's got the whole world in His hands.

3. *He's got the little bitty babies in His hands,*
He's got the little bitty babies in His hands,
He's got the little bitty babies in His hands,
He's got the whole world in His hands.

4. *He's got everybody here in His hands,*
He's got everybody here in His hands,
He's got everybody here in His hands,
He's got the whole world in His hands.

As this song is being sung, invite each family to bring their Hand Bouquets to the altar. This is their offering. They are giving of themselves—their hands, hearts, and whole beings. Encourage everyone to

visualize themselves as servants for Jesus.

After all the Hand Bouquets are on the altar and everyone is back to their seats, join in prayer. Thank God for all the serving hands on the altar. Thank God for each special and unique person there.

Blessing of families: Have people help each other tie on their SON glasses, pointing out that we want to see the needs of others through the eyes of Christ. Ask family units to spend a few minutes naming some needs they see around their community and some ways they could use their gifts to help.

Directions for the family blessing:

1. Join in a circle as a family unit. Units of one or two individuals should join together so there are at least three people in each group.
2. Put your right hands in the middle. Layer your hands and say: "May God bless us with faith."
3. Put your left hands into the huddle of hands and say, "May God bless us with hope."
4. Move hands to join hands in a circle as you say: "May God bless us with peace."
5. Lift hands and place them on each others shoulders and say: "May God bless us with love."
6. Then keep hands on shoulders, bow your heads, close your eyes and say, "In the Name of the Father, of the Son, and the Holy Spirit. Amen."

7. Next, place right and left hands back into the center—layered like a sports team would—saying very enthusiastically, "PRAAAIIISSSE God!" On the name of "God," every hand is lifted up in praise!

8. Sing this SON Glasses Song (to be sung to the tune of *He's Got the Whole World In his Hands*--new words by Sue Lennartson)

    1. *I'll wear my "SON" glasses to see the world,*
       I'll wear my "SON" glasses to see the world,
       I'll wear my "SON" glasses to see the world,
       Looking with God's love and care.
    2. *I'll listen to my Father before I step,*
       I'll listen to my Father before I step,
       I'll listen to my Father before I step,
       God will guide me on my way.
    3. *I'll share the Good, Good News with my voice,*
       I'll share the Good, Good News with my voice,
       I'll share the Good, Good News with my voice,
       Jesus Christ the Son of God.

9. Ask one family to say: "Go in Peace. Serve the Lord." The whole group should then respond by saying: "Thanks be to God."

Explain the Family Devotion sheet is for families with children to take home. Remind them that we are all Christian educators in our homes.

Thank everyone for coming!

FAMILY DEVOTIONS

LIVING THE GOOD NEWS—FAMILY STYLE

Dear Parents:

Please take time for this journey with your family. Use the activities suggested here and adapt them as you need to to make them understandable for your children.

Beginning

Gather as a family with a candle at the center of your gathering space. Light the candle as you say: "In the name of the Father, and of the Son, and of the Holy Spirit."

Bible time

Read aloud Mark 10:13-16 and Luke 18:15-17. Work together to memorize Mark 10:14b. Talk about how Jesus wanted to teach everyone, that he loved families, and loved gathering with children. He showed us his wonderful welcoming spirit.

Discuss or draw a picture

1. How do we as a family welcome people into our home? (Play, meals, parties, Bible study, etc.)
2. How do we make people feel when they come into our home? (Welcomed, fun, stressed, comfortable, uncomfortable?)
3. How do we reach out to each other in our family? (Say I love you, I need and want to spend time with you, and my heart is always a welcoming place for you.)

Music

Following your discussion time, sing a song together. Try *Jesus Loves Me* or another Sunday school or camp song.

Prayer

Your Family Prayer Circle will be an incredible memory for all your family members and strengthen them to live with integrity to their faith values.

Now join hands as a family and pray together. Thank God for the day. Thank God for your family—each person by name. Ask God to help all of you to have a Christ-like welcoming spirit wherever you journey.

If you've never held hands as a family and prayed out loud together, this may feel a bit awkward at first. But the more we pray together, the more incredible the journey!

Serving

Close by blowing out the candle. Remind everyone that we are called to be people of T.I.M.E.–We are **T**otally **i**n **M**ission **E**verywhere!